Teaching

YOUNG WRITERS TO CRAFT

Realistic Fiction

Ready-to-Use Lessons, Mentor Texts, & Ongoing Assessments

Jenny Mechem Bender

Foreword by Carl Anderson

New York • Toronto • London • Auckland • Sydney
Mexico City • New Delhi • Hong Kong • Buenos Aires

Dedication

For my parents, Suzanne and Harvey, who first encouraged me to write.

And for my children, Sophie and Harrison—my most beloved little storytellers.

Cover Designer: Brian LaRossa
Editor: Lois Bridges
Copy/Production Editor: Danny Miller
Interior Designer: Sarah Morrow

Copyright © 2012 by Jenny Mechem Bender
All rights reserved. Published by Scholastic Inc.
Printed in the U.S.A.
ISBN: 978-0-545-28509-4

2   3   4   5   6   7   8   9   10   23   18   17   16   15   14   13   12

Contents

Acknowledgments

I was seven years old when my mother gave me my first writing space, offering her office closet as my own personal refuge. Almost 30 years later, my father makes me feel like I really am a writer every time he encourages me to take a leave from my job (with a beautiful disregard for my mortgage and two children to raise) and devote myself to my passion. I have had more support and encouragement than most have in several lifetimes, and for that, I am forever grateful to a wide berth of people. I especially want to thank those who have directly impacted the creation of this book.

My deepest gratitude goes to Lois Bridges, editor extraordinaire, for being generous (even before there was a book) with her wisdom, praise, and time. If only everyone had someone like Lois at their heels. I also want to thank my production editor, Danny Miller, for his helpful guidance on the book.

I want to thank all the Northampton public school teachers in our realistic fiction study group: Mary Bates, Karen Bryant, Marcia Ciaschini (you are missed), Nancy Harlow, Hannah Kristek, Mary Jo Nagle, and Mary Ellen Reed. They opened their classrooms to me, and they helped me hone and revise my ideas with their own insightful teaching, reflection, and feedback.

Thank you, also, to all the young writers with whom I have the great privilege to work. They are my most brilliant teachers.

I am indebted to my writing partner, Mary Cowey, for reading the manuscript with incredible thought, helping me restructure and clarify from beginning to end. I am also indebted to my dearest friend, Maggie Bittel, for her critical feedback and laugh-out-loud comments in the margins.

Though I no longer work at the Teachers College Reading and Writing Project, it is the learning community that raised me, and I continue to be grateful to everyone there. I am especially grateful to Lucy Calkins for inviting me in and for continuing to support me in the years since I've left. And to Christine Holley and Maura Kaunitz, with whom I first planned a workshop on teaching realistic fiction, which laid the foundation for this book.

I also want to thank Christine, along with Leslie Richmond, for pouring through picture books with me. I am grateful to have life-long colleagues who are also lifelong friends. Thank you to Pam Allyn for putting me in touch with my gift of an editor and to Carl Anderson for making himself available to me whenever I need the wisdom of a mentor.

I am forever grateful for my parents, who have always encouraged me to imagine my dreams into being. Just as I am forever grateful for all the children in my life, especially my own Harrison and Sophie Sewell, for showing me *how* to imagine with commitment and passion and wild creativity.

And of course there is Josh, my love, who supports me with more grace and consistency and patience and (I have to use the word again) *love* than I would ever think possible. Thank you.

Foreword

by Carl Anderson

I first attempted to teach fiction to students in the early 1990s, when I was still a classroom teacher. Although my students had a blast with the unit, I still cringe when I think of the writing they produced. Unlike the beautiful and often powerful personal narratives that they had written previously, their fiction was simply horrible!

The fault didn't really lie with my students, of course, but with me. I just didn't know that much about teaching fiction and, without strong guidance from me, my students muddled through the unit the best that they could.

How I wish I had a copy back then of Jenny Bender's *Teaching Young Writers to Craft Realistic Fiction*. Jenny's extensive knowledge about teaching fiction to youngsters, gained from her many years of being a teacher and staff developer, would have helped me teach fiction with clarity and rigor.

This book is one of the best descriptions of how to teach fiction that I have encountered in the field of teaching writing. And, not only that, it is one of the most clearly written explanations of how to do a genre study that I have read. This book transcends its subject, and will help teachers not only to teach fiction well, but also to be better writing teachers across the entire year.

So many aspects of this book excite me. I love the numerous suggestions for teaching points that Jenny makes for each part of a realistic fiction unit, all nicely aligned with the rigorous expectations for young writers in the Common Core Standards. I love the recommendations of mentor texts that Jenny makes, and how she shows how they can each be used to teach the qualities of good fiction writing. And I especially love the examples of student writing that Jenny includes, which show the results of the strong, knowledgeable teaching that she describes throughout the book.

And there's one final thing that I love about this book: it reminds us how important it is to nurture and support the imagination of primary children. When teachers teach fiction in the way that Jenny Bender describes in this book, they'll be giving students tools for deepening their imaginative capabilities. And that may be the most important contribution that this book makes to the lives of the many children who will be touched by it.

Introduction

Harrison, my five-year-old son, has long been engrossed by fiction, and now, his two-and-a-half-year-old sister, Sophie, is following in his footsteps. They both love to hear a good story and, even at their young ages, they also love to compose a good story. Most days, I overhear them on the floor while I prepare a meal, or sitting in their beds while they wait for sleep, talking with their toys and "writing" fiction. Lately, Harrison's stories are about dinosaurs. Last week, Sophie told me a story about a bear that came to visit her in the night. Between the two of them, there are stories about the ocean, about girls who didn't wear their seat belts, about the adventures of someone in Africa.

Of course I think my children are the most special children in the world. And yet, I also know that they are just like most children when it comes to their love of the imaginary world.

For many of us, the increasing pressure to "teach to the test" feels devastating, especially as this pressure moves into younger and younger grades. I would never suggest that primary teachers bring explicit test preparation into their curriculum. What I do suggest is that we continue to seek out the most creative, engaging, developmentally appropriate methods for building a strong literacy foundation since that will, of course, make it easier for our students to meet the standards as they move through the grades.

Teaching students to write realistic fiction means teaching them to write with meaning, focus, and detail; it means teaching them to consider voice and audience as they begin to explore and discover the power of language. The beauty is that children are dying to write fiction. As you read this, you are likely thinking, "I know! My students are always begging to write make-believe stories!" Teaching students to craft realistic stories allows us to honor and engage young minds, as we also help students learn the fundamental qualities of good writing.

How This Book Is Organized

Each chapter in this book focuses on a different stage of a realistic fiction unit, and every chapter includes the following features:

Overview

Before I take you through the specifics of each stage of a realistic fiction unit, I provide a vision of how things might go. Included in this section is a synopsis of the current goals and recommended pacing.

Teaching Points for Whole-Class and Differentiated Instruction

Whenever I pack for a trip, I gather everything I may want to bring with me and lay it across my bed. Then, as I scrutinize weather and potential plans and length of the visit, I begin to pick and choose exactly what will make it into my suitcase. Similarly, before we move into a new phase of a unit, we want to lay out possible lessons before we pick and choose the best menu and sequence for the students before us. The heart of every chapter is a list of possible teaching points for helping your students move through each stage of a realistic fiction unit. Depending on your students, some lessons will feel more appropriate for whole-class instruction and others for individual and small-group work.

Step-by-Step Prompts for Writing Your Own Teaching Texts

I know how much easier it is to teach something when I feel comfortable with the topic. I also know I am much more likely to learn something when the person teaching me demonstrates a personal experience with, and an understanding of, the topic. For both reasons, I strongly encourage writing teachers to write themselves and to use their own writing inside the classroom as demonstration tools. Even when teachers embrace writing, it is often challenging to figure out how to write texts that can be used effectively in the classroom. In this section, I provide easy-to-follow prompts and guidelines for writing your own realistic fiction to be used in your lessons and conferences.

Teaching With Published Texts

As a writer, I know how much published literature can help me create my own powerful pieces of writing. Whenever I am stuck, struggling with how to structure or craft a piece of writing, I turn to the authors on my shelves for guidance and inspiration. I might investigate how they begin a chapter or organize a paragraph or use a certain type of punctuation. The more we share examples of strong writing with our students, the more familiar they are with the look and sound of beautifully crafted text, and the better able they become to write well themselves. In this section, I highlight different ways you might use recommended realistic fiction at each stage of the unit so that your students can better understand the writing qualities you want them to internalize.

Ongoing Assessment

True teaching is a response to the learner's goals and abilities. Even though we always begin a unit of study with a map of how our teaching might go, we should also revise that map as we watch the strengths and needs of our writers shift and change. Before we begin a new series of lessons, we want to reflect on what we've taught thus far to ascertain the best way to proceed, both with our whole class and our differentiated instruction. Each chapter therefore includes sections on ongoing assessment.

Student Writing Samples

Because our students are the ones who ultimately inspire us and give us a vision of what is possible, I weave student writing throughout each chapter. At the end of Chapters 4, 5, 6 and 8, I also include and discuss writing from two students (Ellen and Alexa) from each stage of their realistic fiction units.

Who This Book Is For

This book is for anyone who values the imagination and wants to teach young students to write realistic fiction. I encourage readers to use the information in this book to explore and discover, take risks, and make choices alongside your students. Some of you may want to follow the strategies as they appear in the book, others may focus on a particular section or chapter as you tread new ground; still others may take what I provide and make it into something else beautiful and new. Whatever path you take, I hope you and your students find meaning and inspiration, and new ways to honor and celebrate the creative mind.

CHAPTER 1

Getting Ready for the Unit

I remember the first time I taught my second grade students to write fiction. I was as excited as they were to make up characters and explore possible plots, and I couldn't wait to read what their eager, imaginative minds produced. But the more I read their stories, the more my heart sank. In part, I was disheartened by events like Mark's car bombs, Alexis's alien invasions, and Samantha's cats that flew and talked simply for the sake of flying and talking. Mostly I was disheartened because with or without the aliens and flying cats, my students were writing stories that went on and on and on without focus, without any believable characters, and without any real purpose or meaning. For anyone who has taught realistic fiction, you know the pitfalls—from writing stories full of overly dramatic, unbelievable events to writing stories devoid of any plot at all. Because of the challenges, many teachers shy away from teaching their students to write fiction.

However, because teaching fiction well means teaching the qualities of good writing while also honoring our students' hunger for make-believe, I encourage all teachers to experiment with fiction in their classrooms. In this chapter, I outline four things we should do *before* beginning a realistic fiction unit that will pave the way for success. Section I includes activities we might do all year long, even if we won't teach fiction until April or May, and Section II includes things to do closer to beginning a fiction unit.

I. Activities All Year Long

Teach Students to Tell and Write True Stories

As a classroom teacher, I always began the year with storytelling. I shared my own stories—perhaps the story of when Wendy and Hera made fun of the new white dress I was so excited to wear to school and never wore again after that day. Or the story of when my best friend cut her doll's hair and blamed it on me. Or the story of getting my first pet, a rat I named Pickle, who liked to nibble on my hair. And, of course, I asked students to share their stories. What I came to understand is how important it is to begin with *true* stories (personal narrative), the stories that build community as well as an understanding of narrative.

Every story, true or make-believe, follows a similar structure: characters move through events (often to attain a desire or solve a problem) that impact their internal and/or external world in some way. Every story writer, whether composing fact or fiction, faces similar hurdles: to craft an alluring lead, develop rich characters, show setting, build tension, and come up with a powerful ending. One of the big differences, of course, is that fiction writers have endless possibilities when it comes to content, whereas personal narrative writers are confined by what actually happened.

"Endless possibilities" is one of the things that makes it so difficult to write fiction well. Our youngest writers can so easily get carried away by a story that they often let one action spark another and another until they have crafted a series of unfocused, disconnected events. When we write true stories, we can at least rely on what actually happened for major details about characters and setting, problems and solutions; because the blueprint of the plotline already exists with personal narrative, it is a more accessible genre through which to learn the qualities of good story writing. I therefore encourage educators to teach students to write true stories before teaching them to write make-believe ones.

Because our youngest writers can usually talk more fluently than they can write, we should create opportunities for them to *tell* stories, if not before, then alongside teaching them to write stories. If we begin the year teaching students to write or draw stories of things that have happened to them, we should also teach them how to tell those stories to a partner. We can teach them to tell a story as a way to plan for what they will write or draw as a way to share what they have already put on the page. I believe we should continue a tradition of oral storytelling in our classrooms even as our students become more adept at the written story. Doing so teaches students to use multiple forms of expression, to link the spoken with the written, and to consider and understand audience in very concrete terms. It also creates an environment in which every student knows she will have a chance to share and be listened to, which helps develop oral language as well as confidence and a sense of self-worth.

We can carve out time at different points across our days to encourage storytelling. For many teachers, such as those who use the Responsive Classroom approach, Morning Meeting is a critical practice aimed at building community and giving students time to rehearse social and academic skills. Morning Meeting usually follows a predictable structure that includes a time for sharing. Instead of sharing objects through "show and tell," you might teach students to share and respond to one another's stories (Dousis, 2008).

In addition to or instead of sharing stories during Morning Meeting, you might have students tell stories right after recess or a special as a way to calm and regroup the class before moving into the next part of the day. I often had my students tell stories when we found ourselves with five or ten minutes to spare in between other activities. Other teachers set aside time immediately before writers' workshop when they want to teach a different topic in the mini-lesson but still explicitly link the oral with the written.

Regardless of when you create opportunities for students to tell their stories, keep in mind a few critical points. First, you only need 10 to 15 minutes a few days a week. Also, though you will often have everyone practice telling stories by working with partners, there are times when one student will tell a story to the entire class. Teachers who embed the practice into Morning Meeting often have a new student tell a story each day. Afterward, the rest of the class offers empathic comments and asks questions that encourage the person sharing to clarify or elaborate. For example, in one classroom a listener responded to a story with, "That must have been exciting for you. What was the best thing you and Zoey did?" (Dousis, 2008).

Most importantly, we need to teach students how to tell stories. We need to teach them the qualities of a good narrative, such as developing characters and building tension. But we also need to teach them the qualities of good *speaking*, such as hooking an audience, gauging their attention, and having ways to re-engage them if that attention begins to wane. Similarly, we need to teach the listeners how to listen and respond, which ultimately impacts their knowledge of narrative, as well.

If one student is telling a story for the whole class, your teaching will most likely take the form of coaching; as a student tells a story, you will probably ask questions to elicit qualities of good writing. For example, your prompts might include one or more of the following:

:: "Before you jump to the end of your story, can you tell us what happened in the middle?"

:: "Could you tell us how your characters were feeling when that happened?"

:: "Could you describe where your characters are?"

If the whole class is telling stories simultaneously, your teaching will more likely take the form of direct instruction; you will tell, then show, students what you want them to do before giving them time to practice. You might say something like, "It's important to tell stories in the order that things occurred so that our audience can make sense of what happened. One way to do this is to tell the beginning, middle, and end across three fingers, making sure all the parts go together." From there, give students an example by telling a simple, focused story from your own life across three fingers. For example, as I hold up my first finger I might say, "Yesterday, I took my dog Lillie for a long walk." As

I hold up my second finger: "An orange cat ran in front of us, and Lillie tried to chase her." And finally, as I hold up my third finger: "But I said, 'No!' and held on tight to the leash." After I model, I ask everyone to practice telling their partners a story from their lives.

Within a few minutes, you might decide to teach a new strategy; depending on the needs of your students, you might say something like, "It's also important to let readers know how your characters feel. Listen to how I re-tell my same story, but this time, with feeling words in it." After modeling, again ask the class to practice with their partners. Students might revise their oral stories two or three times during the 10 to 15 minutes you've set aside for this practice. Of course, the strategies you focus on will vary from class to class depending on what's most relevant for your particular students to lift the quality of their storytelling and writing.

Read Aloud and Discuss Fiction

According to Brian Cambourne's "Conditions of Learning," *immersion* is a critical component to learning (Cambourne, 1995). Before asking students to write in a particular genre, I therefore always immerse them in the genre as readers, so they can begin to absorb and understand the sound and feel and structure of whatever it is they are about to create themselves. "It is mainly through *reading* that writers initially learn all the techniques they know. To learn how to write for a newspaper, one must read newspapers; to write poetry, one must read poetry" (Butler and Turbil, 1987, p. 15). So, of course, to write fiction, one must read fiction. Especially with our youngest students who either cannot yet read themselves or cannot read a wide range of texts, the most effective way to expose them to a genre is by reading aloud to them. Some of my favorite picture books to read aloud before and during a realistic fiction unit include:

:: *Tess's Tree*, Jess Brallier
:: *The Curious Garden*, Peter Brown
:: *Fly Away Home*, Eve Bunting
:: *Grandma's Gloves*, Cecil Castellucci
:: *On Meadowview Street*, Henry Cole
:: *Oliver Button Is a Sissy*, Tomie dePaola
:: *How to Heal a Broken Wing*, Bob Graham
:: *Amazing Grace*, Mary Hoffman
:: *A Letter to Amy*, Ezra Jack Keats
:: *Bag in the Wind*, Ted Kooser

- *Wave*, Suzy Lee
- *Busing Brewster*, Richard Michelson
- *The Very Best Pumpkin*, Mark Kimball Moulton
- *The Dot*, Peter H. Reynolds
- *Unique Monique*, Maria Rousaki
- Henry and Mudge series, Cynthia Rylant
- *The Old Woman Who Named Things*, Cynthia Rylant
- *The Tenth Good Thing About Barney*, Judith Viorst
- *Ira Sleeps Over*, Bernard Waber
- *Knuffle Bunny Free*, Mo Willems
- *William's Doll*, Charlotte Zolotow

In addition to reading aloud our favorite chapter books and the books we love for the stories alone, we also want to find and read texts we love that are similar in length and structure and craft to the ones we will soon ask our students to create. Doing so will make it easier for our students to mentor themselves to the published authors on their shelves. Later in this chapter, I talk about how to choose these mentors, and I recommend titles by grade level.

As an elementary school teacher, I usually did two types of read alouds each day: For one, I simply read aloud a text without interruption to expose my students to a great story, poem, or simple nonfiction text, allowing them to sit back and enjoy. But once a day, I also combined conversation with my read aloud for the purpose of scaffolding students' use of critical reading skills, from monitoring for meaning, to inferring, to critical thinking. During these read alouds, I usually stop several times in the midst of reading and again at the end of a text, each time asking students to talk with a partner. At the end of a story (and sometimes in the middle of a story), I usually follow partner talk with whole-class conversation. To initiate conversation about a story, I pose open-ended questions like:

- What are you learning about these characters?
- How does this part make you feel?
- How do you think the characters are feeling?
- Can you picture where this story takes place and describe everything you see?
- What do you think the character(s) might do to try and solve the problem?
- What kind of relationship do these characters have?
- What do you think is fair or unfair in this story?
- How does this story compare with and/or differ from other stories we've read?

Scaffold Student Conversation

When students talk with a partner, they turn to the person next to them to discuss what they're making of text. As students talk with one another, I circulate, listening in on a few conversations. Based on my assessment of individual conversations, I might briefly interject with a prompt aimed at lifting the level of their thinking and talking. For example, if I hear students having a hard time making character inferences, I might say something like, "Readers often put themselves in the characters' shoes to imagine how characters might be feeling or why they might be acting the way they are. Could you try that with this story to help you imagine what these characters might be experiencing?" Or if I hear one student dominating the conversation, I might say something like, "When you have a conversation, it's important to listen to what other people are thinking, because that's one way we get new ideas; sometimes this means we need to hold some of our thinking for later and ask a quieter person, 'What are you thinking about the story?' Could you try that now?"

Similarly, during whole-class conversation, I am careful to scaffold talk without *dominating* talk; I want students to feel like the conversation is theirs and not a question-and-answer session between them and the teacher. When I interrupt whole-class conversation, it is again usually to share a strategy (as I model above) that I think will help improve students' talking or thinking, and then I once again remove myself from the conversation and listen to what students do with the strategy. Or I might interject to name something they have done particularly well that I want them to remember and continue to do whenever they respond to literature and/or to each other.

Another way I facilitate versus dominate conversation is by teaching students to look at each other when they speak, not at me. In the beginning of the year, when I'm still calling on students, I teach them to raise their thumb in front of their chest instead of raising their hand in the air, so as not to distract or intimidate other thinkers in the room. And very soon, I teach them to call on each other by asking the person who just spoke to *quickly* pick the next speaker, whenever possible someone with their thumb up who has not yet spoken.

Scaffolding student conversations about text allows them to make sense of, engage with, and think critically about what is on the page. Once we give students an opportunity to understand and explore what a story is about, we can return to it at a later date and teach students to notice and understand how it is written and how the author uses features of the genre. Doing so lays the foundation for students to do similar work with their own pieces.

II. Getting Ready for a Fiction Unit

I enter into every unit of study with a plan, but I know this plan is always tentative because ultimately, what I teach is a response to the very specific needs of the students before me. In reading this book, you will have your plan for teaching students to write fiction. But before you actually begin the unit (and many times in the midst of the unit), you will want to assess what your particular students understand about crafting story so you can use that information to fine-tune your agenda.

Assess Students' Skills

In the beginning of this chapter, I encourage readers to teach personal narrative prior to teaching fiction. When it comes time to assess students' narrative knowledge, you can return to those pieces, using the qualities of good writing that cut across narrative genres (writes with focus; develops characters and setting; crafts strong leads and endings, and so on) as lenses for assessing their most recent personal narratives. You'll need to make those lenses more specific if there are certain strategies you want to assess—for example, you might break apart "develops characters" into a list of strategies your writers might use to develop their characters: feeling words, speech bubbles, body movements, dialogue, and so on. You'll also want to assess your students' current use of spacing, punctuation, and spelling so you can choose one or two developmentally appropriate convention goals for your fiction unit. Make sure you assess stories that reflect what your students do *independently*; in other words, try to look at stories that your students have written (and possibly revised and edited) without much assistance from you. You might use something like the template in Figure 1.1 to organize your assessment (see the appendix for a reproducible, as well as a blank assessment template).

As you assess your writers, consider the level at which they have internalized each skill; you might jot "N" when there is no evidence of a skill, "E" when a skill is emerging, and "I" when a skill has been internalized.

Again, your assessment will drive your planning. For example, if the majority of your students show no evidence of developing their characters well, you can plan to concentrate on this skill by mapping out several different lessons, probably at different stages of your realistic fiction unit, on ways writers develop characters. If the majority of your students are consistently writing focused stories, you may (or may not) do a review lesson on writing with focus, but you will otherwise concentrate on different skills. (In Chapters 4–6, I include possible lessons on writing with detail and focus, as well as leads and endings.)

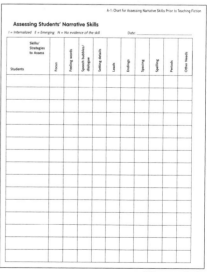

Figure 1.1

Create and Gather Demonstration Texts

As a classroom teacher, I had the good fortune of working alongside some of the most gifted teachers I have ever seen, and the additional fortune of working in truly collaborative communities where we were always in and out of one another's classrooms. When I wasn't making copies for my next period or dealing with some student's emergency, I spent my preparation periods in a colleague's classroom, watching her teach and learning new strategies for managing a challenging class or teaching an engaging lesson. If you are like me, you learn through seeing.

Because demonstration is a critical condition of learning (Cambourne, 1995), I always show students examples of what I want them to do as writers. In any unit of study, this means gathering, both from published and student writers, examples of the various strategies I plan to teach, as well as creating my own written examples. I always encourage teachers to draw from all three of these sources (published, student, and self). Using our favorite published texts usually means exposing students to the most beautifully crafted literature; it also helps connect their reading and writing in more explicit ways. Using student samples means exposing students to what is truly possible; it also teaches them to learn from and value one another. Creating our own examples means exposing students to their teacher as a writer and a learner, just like them; it sends the message that we are in this work together, challenges and all, which helps engage students and encourage their own risk-taking.

For every unit I teach, I choose one to two published texts I know I can use again and again to teach a variety of lessons; these become our class mentor texts. At times, I may pull another text from my shelves to teach something I cannot exemplify with my mentor, but it is easier for me and for my students when I can rely most heavily on the same one or two texts. When choosing mentor texts, I consider four key characteristics: length, level, language, and love. I pick texts that are close to the length of what my students will be writing—so no chapter books! I look for texts on the easier side so students can access them as readers, if not independently, then with assistance; I also want them to be able to access the texts as *writers* by noticing and trying certain elements of the craft. By language, I mean that I look for texts written in ways I want to teach my students to write; for example, if I want to teach my students to develop characters and build tension, I look for published texts that demonstrate this well. Finally, I look for texts that my students and I love since we will be returning to them again and again.

Below is a list of possible mentors organized by grade. Because several could also be used as mentor texts when we teach personal narrative, we need to decide at the beginning of the year which texts we'll use in each unit so we're certain to have separate examples. Though we might use the same text to teach personal narrative one year and realistic fiction the next, doing so in the same year will confuse our teaching and students' understanding.

In most cases, anything that is appropriate for a lower grade would also be appropriate for the next grade or two above. However, in an effort to differentiate instruction in a building where teachers across grades might study realistic fiction, I suggest kindergarten and first grade teachers get first choice of the easiest texts. In general, you may find many of the stories I suggest for one grade also feel appropriate for your grade, but again, discuss your choices with colleagues in the building to ensure students do not receive the same instruction from year to year.

Kindergarten

- :: *When Sophie Gets Angry—Really, Really Angry . . .*, Molly Bang
- :: *Sophie's Big Bed*, Tina Burke
- :: *Julius's Candy Corn*, Kevin Henkes*
- :: *Lilly's Chocolate Heart*, Kevin Henkes*
- :: *Sheila Rae's Peppermint Stick*, Kevin Henkes*
- :: *The Carrot Seed*, Ruth Krauss
- :: *Bunny Cakes*, Rosemary Wells*
- :: *Timothy Goes to School*, Rosemary Wells*
- :: *Knuffle Bunny*, Mo Willems
- :: *Knuffle Bunny Too*, Mo Willems

1st Grade

- :: *The Sandwich Swap*, Her Majesty Queen Rania Al Abdullah
- :: *Bailey Goes Camping*, Kevin Henkes*
- :: *Jessica*, Kevin Henkes*
- :: *Owen*, Kevin Henkes*
- :: *My Friend and I*, Lisa Jahn-Clough
- :: *Goggles*, Ezra Jack Keats
- :: *Peter's Chair*, Ezra Jack Keats
- :: *Ruthie and the (Not So) Teeny Tiny Lie*, Laura Rankin*
- :: *The Stray Dog*, Marc Simont
- :: *Caps for Sale*, Esphyr Slobodkina

* Though the pictures in these texts depict all the characters as animals, the words allow us to envision realistic people behaving in realistic ways. When I use these books as mentors, I always have a conversation first with students about how the stories are realistic if we look beyond the pictures. "Let's imagine for a moment that we replaced all of these pictures with ones of boys and girls and men and women," I might say to students. "If I did that in a book like The Three Little Pigs, *the story still wouldn't feel realistic because it would show people doing unbelievable things, like a man blowing down a family's house with his breath—that isn't really believable! But in this book, if we put in new pictures, we would see everyday people doing everyday things, like [getting teased at school or fighting with a sibling]." If, despite such an explanation, you still think your students would be confused about what makes fiction realistic, choose a different mentor text; we do not want to inadvertently encourage students to write stories about talking animals!*

2nd Grade

- :: *Melissa Parkington's Beautiful, Beautiful Hair*, Pat Brisson

- :: *Sheila Rae the Brave*, Kevin Henkes*
- :: *Horace and Morris Join the Chorus (But What About Dolores?)*, James Howe
- :: *Goal!*, Mina Javaherbin
- :: *King of the Playground*, Phyllis Reynolds Naylor
- :: *Whistling*, Elizabeth Partridge
- :: *Ruby and the Copy Cat*, Peggy Rathman
- :: *Ish*, Peter H. Reynolds
- :: *My Best Friend*, Mary Ann Rodman
- :: *Big Sister and Little Sister*, Charlotte Zolotow

As I gather published texts, I also gather student samples I've collected over the years that I know I might use to model certain predictable strategies. Don't worry if you do not yet have a collection of student fiction; as soon as your kids start writing, you can start gathering samples and using them as models for the rest of your class.

Sam's Selfish

Sam was walking in the park with his scooter. His friend came over and asked him if he could have a turn on his scooter, but he said, "No."

Ben felt sad and angry. He walked away. Sam felt ashamed of himself.

Sam went over to his friend and said, "You can borrow my scooter for a day and let me borrow your bike for a day."

Ben said, "Sure, I'll go get my bike."

"Okay," said Sam. They were friends forever.

Figure 1.2—Jackson's realistic fiction piece, first grade

As an example, I could use the student story in Figure 1.2 to teach the following:

:: To make sure we write focused pieces, we usually plan our stories. One way to plan is to say and sketch each part across pages, making sure we have a clear beginning, middle, and end; then we can write down our words.

:: One way to write with more detail and pull our readers inside our stories is to stretch the beginning, middle, and end across pages; often, writers even stretch the middle of our stories over more than one page.

:: Writers often create a title that connects with an idea in our piece because it gets readers ready to understand what our story is about.

:: One way to make sure our stories are focused is to make sure every part (and every page) somehow connects with the problem and solution.

:: When we write realistic fiction, we write about believable yet make-believe characters, who face an everyday problem and eventually find an everyday solution.

:: It is important to let readers know how characters feel about events, so our readers know how *they* should feel; one way to do this is to simply tell the feeling.

:: Writers often use speech bubbles to show what is happening in the story and to create voice.

:: Writers often use dialogue (we write the exact words that characters say) to show instead of tell important events in our stories.

:: When writers use dialogue, we put quotes (talking marks) at the beginning and at the end of *just those words coming out of a character's mouth,* so our readers know a character is speaking.

:: Writers let readers know the setting of our stories (where stories take place). We can tell readers where characters are; we can also put details in our pictures that let readers know where characters are.

:: Writers often end stories by letting readers know what has changed or what happens as result of the change.

:: When writers edit our stories, we carefully read them out loud to make sure everything makes sense. Sometimes, we realize we left out a word, in which case we can use a caret to indicate where to add it.

In addition to gathering published and student samples, I begin to think about the writing samples *I* might create to use as models for what I want my students to do. I remind myself who I am writing for: five or six or seven year olds. I choose topics relevant to their lives, topics that might spark their own writing ideas; for example, I might write a make-believe story about a little girl who is teased at school or about a little boy who is afraid of the dark. I also try to write slightly above where the majority of my students are writing. As with published texts, I want to show my students examples of strong writing that are within their zone of proximal development (Vygotsky, 1978, 86), knowing that something too simple or too sophisticated will fail to scaffold their learning. In the chapters that follow, I offer more explicit support for creating model texts at each stage of a fiction unit.

Gather Student Writing Materials

I strongly encourage primary teachers to have students write on individual sheets of paper and to keep their writing inside their own two-pocket folders. Unlike notebooks, individual pages allow us to better support the different developmental stages of writers in a class; depending on the writer (or on the task at hand), we can encourage them to choose paper with no lines at all, with just a couple of lines, or with many lines; we can also offer paper with thinner and with thicker spaces between lines to support writers as they transition from writing larger to smaller print. Writing on individual pages also makes it easier for students to revisit earlier drafts; unlike with a notebook, students can cut and rearrange the order of parts, insert new pieces of paper to stretch middle parts of a story, and add more to a draft written days or weeks prior. (For these same reasons, I teach students to only write on one side of the page.) In most classrooms, extra paper is kept in a writing center along with other tools writers may need: date stamps, tape, scissors, staplers, pens and pencils, and sticky notes. (See the appendix for some of the paper choices we might offer primary students.)

On the first day of a unit, I always choose one type of paper to put inside every writing folder to avoid "traffic jams" at the writing center. But students know that whenever they need new paper, they can independently walk to the writing center and choose it themselves. Over the course of the unit, I might introduce new types of paper to better support the type of work I teach the class to do, or to better support the amount of text students are beginning to produce.

Envision the Big Picture

Stage 1: Developing a Vision of the Genre

2–3 days (Chapters 2 and 3)

:: Teacher continues to read aloud and discuss realistic fiction.

:: Students revisit short, realistic fiction. As a class and with partners, they notice everything they can about the genre and how authors structure and craft their stories. Teacher and students chart their observations.

:: Teacher leads the class through a shared writing of a realistic fiction story.

Stage 2: Generating Topics and Planning

5–7 days (Chapter 4)

:: Students create and develop possible characters for their stories.

:: Students generate possible problems for their characters.

:: Students generate possible solutions for those problems.

:: Students plan their stories before drafting.

Stage 3: Drafting and Revising

6–8 days (Chapters 5–7)

:: Students write with focus.

:: Students develop characters and possibly the setting.

:: Students stretch out problems and solutions to build tension.

:: Students consider thoughtful leads and/or endings.

:: Students attend to conventions as they draft.

:: If students have more than one draft, they pick one to publish.

:: Students revise for focus and detail.

Stage 4: Editing, Publishing, and Celebrating

3–4 days (Chapter 8)

:: Students edit their pieces with attention to meaning and conventions.

:: Students finish and color illustrations; they might practice reading their pieces aloud.

:: The class celebrates the pieces they've published by sharing them with an audience.

Beginning a new unit of study always feels like a risk, like I'm standing on the edge of a diving board, excited to plunge into the water but nervous about landing on my belly or back. As teachers, we know the feeling of landing on our bellies and backs, of staring out at a sea of confused faces or seeing no evidence of student growth after what we thought was our best teaching. But we also know the feeling of a perfect dive, of doing a lesson and watching our students rush back to their seats excited and engaged, of reading a piece of writing and seeing the footprints of our teaching all over the page. My hope is that the above suggestions will give you the confidence you need to plunge head-first into teaching realistic fiction, and that it will give you the tools you need to experience some perfect dives as you and your students make your way through the unit.

CHAPTER 2

Developing a Vision of the Genre

Starting a realistic fiction unit is a bit like being a rock star and walking onto a concert stage: in both cases, the crowd usually erupts in a wave of cheers and claps. Finally the time has come to write make-believe stories! However, before students actually sit down to write, I want them to have a clear understanding of what it is I want them to make, as well as a vision of how that work will unfold.

Though most of our students have been reading (or listening to) realistic fiction for years, they may not have formed an explicit understanding of the difference between realistic fiction and other types of stories. Even when their knowledge of realistic fiction is more developed, immersing them in the genre allows students to notice new things they might try as writers. And even if they have written realistic fiction before, giving them a big-picture vision of how to craft their stories helps them develop new understandings as they move through the unit, and it helps them produce more successful pieces.

Overview

During this stage of the unit, which will likely last two to three days, I have two primary goals:

1. Teaching students to read as writers for the purpose of better understanding the genre
2. Crafting a shared realistic fiction story with the class to give students a vision of the work they will soon do independently (Chapter 3)

Below are several strategies you might use to help attain these goals. Though there will not be time to cover everything during whole-class mini-lessons, you might find some of the following teaching topics appropriate for differentiated instruction and for middle- and end-of-the-workshop teaching.

Create a Predictable Writing Workshop Structure

I begin each writing block by gathering the class in a meeting area for a mini-lesson that teaches something most of the students need to learn. I keep my lesson short, about 10 minutes, so students have plenty of time for independent practice.

After the mini-lesson, students return to their seats and their independent writing. While students work, I differentiate my instruction through one-on-one conferences and small-group strategy lessons, during which I tailor my teaching to meet individual needs.

Often, I stop students in the midst of their independent writing for brief teaching (usually a couple of minutes) aimed at providing additional support—again, something that would benefit the majority of students. With students still in their seats, I might do any of the following: highlight student work that exemplifies my teaching in the mini-lesson; briefly re-teach part of my mini-lesson; give students time to share and reflect with a partner; extend the lesson by introducing something slightly new to consider; remind students to keep practicing something they've learned earlier in the unit or year (for example, spacing or periods); or teach toward a writing habit or process that cuts across genre (for example, logistical revision practices or noise level).

In some classrooms, especially toward the beginning of the year when students are not yet accustomed to writing for extended periods of time, I might weave multiple mid-workshop teachings throughout the writing block. Doing so gives students breaks from their independent writing and helps them build their stamina. After my mid-workshop teaching, students return to their own writing.

I conclude every writing workshop with a share (which usually lasts between two and seven minutes) aimed at providing closure to the day's work. Though most young writers clamor for the chance to read their pieces aloud to the class, I teach students early in the year that, as with middle-of-the-workshop teaching, the end of workshop is usually a time to share and reflect with a partner, or it is a time to highlight work from two or three students who successfully tried something I want the rest of the class to learn. In the latter case, I choose students based on the strategies they tried that day. Rather than read their entire pieces, students share just those sections that exemplify my teaching. I use my conference notes to keep track of who has shared so that I can make sure everyone's work is highlighted over the course of a unit, not just the most confident and successful writers; to achieve this goal, I might help a student accomplish something during a conference and then highlight their success to the whole class.

Learning to Read as Writers

Because "knowledge of all the conventions of writing can only come from reading," (Smith, 1994, 195) one of our key roles is to teach students how to read as writers. Whenever I teach students how to write in a new genre, we spend at least the first couple of days revisiting texts we have already read and discussed as readers, so we can begin to identify and chart the things we now notice as writers.

Possible Mini-Lessons to Help Students Read as Writers

According to the Common Core State Standards, kindergarten students should recognize common genre, including stories; by first grade, they should distinguish between genre, and by second grade, they should identify core elements of common genre (Common Core Standards, 2010). When students read realistic fiction as writers, it familiarizes them with the genre and exposes them to all the characteristics of the genre. Furthermore, it gives students a sense of ownership and independence, as they uncover for themselves what they might also do as writers.

Notice all the details about realistic fiction

I introduce reading as writers in my first whole-class lesson by teaching the following: *When we read as readers, we pay attention to what is happening in a story: what the characters' names are, what kind of people they are, what they do, and so on. When we read as writers, we pay attention to how authors make their stories: the kinds of details they include, what they do to get us information about the characters. Before writers write in a new genre, we usually study some experts first—authors who have already written and maybe even published texts in that genre. We notice everything we can about what these authors do, so we can learn what kinds of things we can and should do when we start writing.*

I usually model this concept by asking students to watch as I look between two or three familiar stories and say things like, "One of the first things I notice is that this book has a title on the front cover . . . and look, so do these. Let me write that on our chart. What else do I notice? Well, when I open to the first page, I see pictures of tall buildings. I don't think it's so important that there are tall buildings because that has to do with what this particular story is about and not how it is written; I *do* think it's important that I see where the story takes place—in a city, which is where we find tall buildings like these. I wonder if these other books have information in them about where the stories take place . . ."

Once I model, I might ask students to practice the strategy with a partner: "I gave each partnership two familiar realistic fiction books to bring to the mini-lesson. I want all of you to practice reading as writers by noticing one or two things the author or illustrator of each books does."

Create a Consistent Mini-Lesson Structure

In every mini-lesson, which I try to keep to 10 minutes or under so students have plenty of time for their independent writing, I do three critical things:

1. I tell students what I want them to learn. I try to be as specific as possible by naming the skill (which is another word for my end goal) as well as a strategy or two students can use to practice this goal. In the above example, the skill is reading as writers and the strategy is noticing everything and anything that authors do.

2. After I tell students what I want them to learn, I show them. I use published, student, or my own writing (or in the above example, my own process of thinking about writing) to exemplify my teaching.

3. Finally, I ask students to briefly practice my teaching before they return to their desks. Most days, my mini-lesson is *not* a directive for the entire class to follow immediately. Rather, it is something students will practice when it is in their zone of proximal development *and* when it is relevant to their current work. For example, when I teach strategies for ending a piece, I know there will be a handful of students who have more pressing needs, while others may have just begun a piece and hence need to wait a day or two before practicing what I just taught. Especially because I usually do not expect everyone to practice the mini-lesson when they return to their seats, I give students a couple of minutes to practice inside the mini-lesson as a first step toward internalizing my teaching. I also make running charts of key skills and strategies and hang them in the room (trying not to hang more than 2 to 3 charts at a time so as not to overwhelm students), so both independently and with my direction, students can refer to them when relevant.

After we quickly share some of what students notice, I wrap up the lesson with a reminder of the teaching point and with any final directions; for example, in this case, I let students know I have already stacked several familiar fiction books at every table. When I send students back to their seats, they spend the rest of workshop looking at and discussing with a partner or a small group everything they notice inside the pages of those books. Because I have already spent weeks reading realistic fiction aloud to students, I have been modeling the kind of language we might use to describe such texts. Even in kindergarten and first grade classrooms where the students likely cannot read the books independently, they are familiar enough with the genre and the specific stories that they can notice things like, "All these books have characters in them!" And, "I know there is a problem in this story because I remember that the bird hurt its wing." Other critical features students often notice, whether or not they can read, include details in the pictures; different types of punctuation marks on the page (whether or not they know what they are called); different types of print

What We Notice
About Realistic Fiction

- *Relationships*
- *Characters*
- *Important people and stuff*
- *Titles*
- *Sound words*
- *Characters do things*
- *Lots of punctuation like ! … " " ? ( ) [ ]*
- *Some words are all capitals*
- *Problems*
- *Solutions*
- *Characters have feelings*
- *Sometimes no words*
- *Pictures*
- *Pictures show how characters feel*
- *Feelings can change/different feelings in same book*

Figure 2.1

like words in bold or all capitals or italics. In classrooms where students cannot independently read texts and/or it is time-consuming for them to take notes, I generally ask them to put sticky notes on pages where they notice something. By second grade, I might ask one student to jot the group's observations on a piece of paper. At the end of workshop, students can share their observations, and the teacher can make a chart like the one from a kindergarten class shown in Figure 2.1.

Notice craft versus content

When students are first learning how to read as writers, they often focus on what the story is about instead of how it is written. When I circulate the room and hear students say things like, "I notice the boy in this story is sad," I might respond, "Are you saying that a character in this story feels something? I wonder if that's true in other realistic fiction books. Can you see if it's true about these two stories?" Once they see that yes, other stories have characters with feelings, I might say, "So even if I didn't want to write about a boy who is sad, I could write about a character who has feelings. As you keep noticing things, see if you can focus less on what the stories are about and more on what the authors do that you might try, no matter what you are writing about." If a majority of students continue to focus on content over craft, we may need tomorrow's mini-lesson to teach the difference between reading as a reader and reading as a writer. After introducing our teaching point, we might model and then have students practice by sorting several observations into "content" and "craft" categories.

Notice what is true of all realistic fiction and what is true of some

Once students grasp the concept of reading as writers and are easily gathering lists of observations, they can begin to sort their observations. Because our goal is to better understand the genre we are studying, we can ask students to consider what makes something realistic fiction. Either as the focus of a lesson or as a prompt to scaffold independent work after a lesson, we can introduce one or more of the following inquiry questions to individual tables or to the entire class:

- Now that you've noticed so many different characteristics of these stories, could you try to find out which are true of *all* realistic fiction and which are true of *some*? For example, you've noticed that this author includes information about where the story takes place (we call that setting). Could you see whether that's true of these other stories, so we have a better idea whether *every* realistic fiction writer does that?
- How does the book you're looking at compare with or differ from other realistic fiction you've heard or read?

:: If you've noticed something about one story, can you see whether it's true of some other stories as well?

:: What seems to be true of *every* realistic fiction story? What are you finding in only *some* of the stories?

Notice specific elements of realistic fiction

I want students to notice some of the critical elements I plan to teach in the upcoming weeks. For example, I know I will teach the whole class that we are writing *realistic* fiction, and so I want them to notice that even though all the stories we're reading are make-believe, everything in them *could* really happen. I will also teach them that stories follow a similar structure that includes at least one character, problem, and solution.

If students are not independently noticing these text characteristics, I could coach one or two tables, so they can later share their observations with the rest of the class. I might remind them of previous conversations we have had by saying something like, "Do you remember when we talked about how stories usually have a similar pattern? How every story we've read so far included some of the same things?" Or I might say, "I notice that in this story the girl gets lost and in this story the bird breaks its wing and in this story the boy tries to run away from home. Even though they're all about different things, there is something similar happening, a pattern that I think we can say is true about all stories . . . what do you think it is?"

Of course, there are times when the best thing I can do is simply tell students what I want them to notice. As a general rule, when I already know what answer I want, I won't spend much more than a minute trying to get them to name it. Instead, I'll encourage them to keep noticing patterns, saying something like, "What I'm noticing is that so far, all of these stories have at least one big problem in them. I wonder if that's true of these other stories or if it's only true of some stories. Would you look through some other books and let me know what you find? As you're looking, see if you notice any other patterns . . . what else might all these stories have in common?"

Notice what makes a text realistic fiction

If we want to extend the conversations about genre, we can ask students to consider everything they've learned so far to help them define and recognize realistic fiction. We might pose one or more of the following inquiry questions to individual groups or to the entire class:

:: What makes these texts realistic fiction?

:: How is realistic fiction different than other genres we've read (like nonfiction informational books, personal narrative, fantasy, and so on)?

:: I'm going to put some other texts on your tables now, only some of which are realistic fiction. Can you make two piles, one of realistic fiction and one of other genres? As you work, it's important to talk about *why* you're putting something in a certain pile.

Notice how authors accomplish a particular goal, such as character development

Some students quickly grasp the concept of reading as writers and do so with great insight. If I'm looking to challenge students who have already noticed critical features of the genre, I might encourage them to notice *how* authors craft those features. When students notice that all the stories have characters in them, I could push them further by saying, "That is such an important observation because we cannot have a story without characters. Now that you've discovered that, could you look for the different kinds of details authors often include about the characters? For example, I know authors often include how the characters feel. What other information do they share with their readers to help us get to know the characters?"

If most of the class seems ready for the challenge, we might explicitly teach toward one of the following inquiry questions in a mini-lesson, or we might use a mid-workshop interruption to introduce the inquiry question:

:: What type of information do these authors give us about the characters?

:: How do authors let us know about the characters in their stories?

:: How do authors let us know where their stories take place?

Using Published Texts to Teach Students to Read as Writers

For this first stage of a realistic fiction unit, we want to gather our mentor texts as well as other short, realistic fiction we have read with our students. In the previous chapter, I explained my guidelines for choosing mentor texts. I also shared some of my favorite realistic fiction stories to read aloud and to study as writers. Because students are noticing everything they can about realistic fiction, all we need to do during these first few days is highlight for students a few examples of what they might observe. Perhaps we will look at two of three texts and notice that they all have characters in them. Note that even though the characters are make-believe, they still feel like they could be real people who experience real emotions. Perhaps we will also begin to notice what is true of some but not all realistic fiction—for example, that characters talk to each other in some stories but not all. We might also notice different ways authors develop their characters: by including their feelings, their facial expressions, their actions, and their words.

Preparing Our Own Writing to Teach Students How to Read as Writers

Since students are not yet writing, neither do we need to use our own samples during this phase of the unit. Of course, because we always want to be one step ahead of them, we will want to prepare the writing described in the next chapter before teaching our class to do so.

Assessing Students' Understanding of Reading as Writers

During these first days of the unit, we will informally assess students' key understandings as they talk with one another about their observations. The following questions can help scaffold for continued understanding.

Can students read as writers or are they too focused on content?

:: Continue to model your own observations as a writer. When you observe an aspect of a writer's craft, ask students to look through other texts and sort them into two piles: 1) which texts have similar features; and 2) which do not.

:: Make a two-column chart with examples of reading as a *reader* on one side ("I notice this story is about a girl who gets angry a lot.") and parallel examples of reading as a *writer* on the other side ("I notice these stories have characters in them." And "I notice a lot of feelings in these stories.") Help students see how the observations in each pair are similar and connected, but that one type of observation could give a writer ideas no matter what she writes about, whereas the other type of observation describes one thing a story could be about.

:: Record on sticky notes or index cards several different examples of reading as a writer and reading as a reader. Help students sort them into the appropriate categories, asking them to explain their thinking as they work.

Do students understand the critical features of realistic fiction, namely that it includes believable yet make-believe characters, problems, and solutions?

:: Continue to name these three critical features with children and to show them examples from familiar stories.

:: Share familiar texts that do not include these features, from nonfiction texts to stories that are not realistic, like *The Three Little Pigs* or *Frog and Toad*. Show them how these texts incorporate very different features and are therefore not realistic fiction. For example, we might share nonfiction texts that contain lists of facts rather than characters moving through events; we might share fantastical stories like *The Three Little Pigs* to show unrealistic characters and events, such as talking animals that blow down houses.

:: Help students sort texts into appropriate piles: realistic fiction and non-realistic fiction. Ask them to explain their thinking as they work.

CHAPTER 3

Writing Shared Text

The purpose of shared writing is to scaffold for students the work we ultimately want them to do independently. Often, this includes providing a vision for students of the genre in which we want them to write. Shared writing involves creating a piece of text with students while guiding them to use a *range* of writing skills and processes (McKenzie, 1986). For example, during a single, shared writing experience, I might help students decide what to write about, how to plan, what to write first, how to craft a sentence, and so forth. The purpose of a mini-lesson is very different; in a mini-lesson, I explicitly teach toward a *single* skill—for example, one way to get ideas or one way to plan a draft. Though I recommend incorporating shared writing into your week, I don't recommend doing it in lieu of the mini-lesson or independent writing. Shared writing is not technically part of a writing workshop, rather something we do in addition to and in support of workshop.

When I do shared writing with students, I keep it short: between 10 and 20 minutes per session. Though I hold the pen and do all the writing myself, the students craft the ideas (with my guidance).

One of the reasons we teach students to read as writers is to help them internalize a vision of what it is we want them to create themselves. Similarly, writing a realistic fiction piece as a class allows the teacher to quickly guide students through all the major points of the unit, which further helps students to see and understand the big picture before they immerse themselves in their own stories.

To effectively co-create a story with the whole class, you will want two or three 10–15 minute blocks for shared writing. You can write your shared story any time after students have begun to read as writers but before they begin to write their own pieces; for example, you might do shared writing directly after your writing workshop on the first two days of the unit.

One way we might schedule a typical day in kindergarten

Morning Meeting. . . . . .10–15 minutes

Shared Reading. . . . . .10–15 minutes

Snack. . . . . .10–15 minutes

Reading Workshop. . . . . .35–45 minutes

Writing Workshop. . . . . .35–45 minutes

Interactive Writing and/or Word Work. . . . . .10–15 minutes

Lunch and Recess. . . . . .45–50 minutes

Read Aloud with Accountable Talk . . . . .15–20 minutes

Math . . . . .30–40 minutes

Special/Teacher's Prep. . . . . .45–50 minutes

Social Studies or Science. . . . . .30–35 minutes

Snack. . . . . .10–15 minutes

Choice Time . . . . .30–40 minutes

One way we might schedule a typical day in 1st and 2nd grade

Morning Meeting. . . . . .10–15 minutes

Word Work . . . . .10–15 minutes

Shared Reading. . . . . .10–15 minutes

Reading Workshop. . . . . .40–50 minutes

Snack. . . . . .10–15 minutes

Shared or Interactive Writing. . . . . .10–15 minutes

Writing Workshop. . . . . .40–50 minutes

Lunch and Recess. . . . . .45–50 minutes

Read Aloud with Accountable Talk . . . . .15–25 minutes

Math . . . . .50–60 minutes

Science or Social Studies. . . . . .30–35 minutes

Special/Teacher's Prep. . . . . .45–50 minutes

Overview

During our shared writing of a realistic story, I have three primary goals:

1. Provide a vision of how to create a fictional character with believable internal and external traits.

2. Provide a vision of how to generate possible problems and solutions for a realistic fiction story.

3. Provide a vision of how to plan and draft a piece of realistic fiction with a clear beginning, middle, and end.

Unlike the material in the other chapters, I recommend moving through *all* of the teaching topics below in the order I address them.

Interactive writing is similar to shared writing in that teacher and students compose text together. But in interactive writing, the teacher shares the pen, calling on students to record certain parts of the text that is in their zone of development. (McCarrier, Pinnell, and Fountas, 1999)

I. Notice How Another Author Creates a Character, Problem, and Solution

Before we write our own class piece, it helps to spend five to ten minutes studying a beloved realistic fiction story, so we have a blueprint for our own work. First, I remind students that realistic stories contain three critical components:

1. At least one important character
2. who faces at least one problem
3. and finds at least one solution.

Then we chart these characteristics about a book we've read. For example, in one kindergarten class, we talked about *When Sophie Gets Angry—Really, Really Angry . . .* by Molly Bang. First, I asked students, "Who is this story mostly about?"

"Sophie!" they exclaimed. As I drew Sophie's outline, I explained that we usually learn details about how characters are on the inside as well as the outside. Outside details are things we know just by looking at a character: dress, hair color, size, and so on. Inside traits are things we often don't realize about characters until we get to know them better: how they feel, what they want, what they fear. One by one, I ask the class and record their responses to the following questions:

• What is the character like on the outside?

• What is he or she like on the inside?

• What is the big problem the character faces?

• How is the problem solved?

See Figure 3.1 for a character sketch of Sophie.

Figure 3.1

II. Create Our Own Character, Problem, and Solution

Next, I explain that we are going to write our own story, but that first, we need to think of a character, problem, and solution. We start by creating a character, someone around the students' age or younger, so they can really imagine what he or she could be like. Once we choose the gender and a name for our character, I ask students to think about what the character might be like on the outside. As they quietly think, I name some characteristics they might consider: hair, eye, and skin color; size and shape compared to other people their age; typical dress; family; language, and so on. Then I ask them to share their ideas with a partner. When we regroup and share as a class, I record outside traits on our character chart. Then we repeat the process for inside traits: common feelings, fears, wants, favorite people, favorite places, hobbies, strengths, struggles, and so on.

Next, I ask students to think about some problems our character might face, letting the class know that problems might come from something the character wants or fears. I chart a few student suggestions and then quickly vote on the problem we want for this story. Finally, I ask students to consider possible solutions. Again, I chart a few student ideas before we choose the one most like best. Remember, all this happens in 10–15 minutes! See Figure 3.2 for an example.

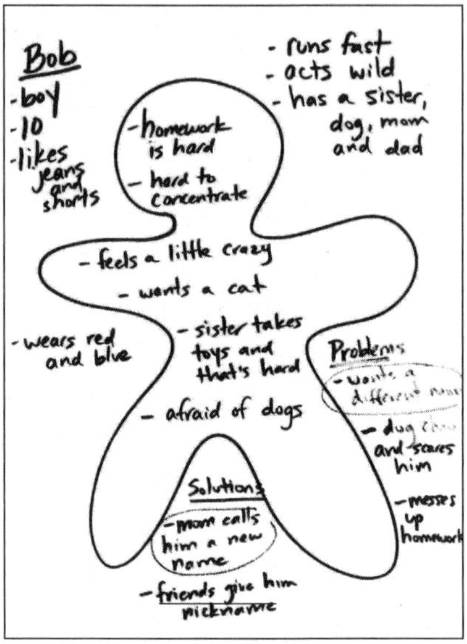

III. Plan and Draft Our Story

Usually on the following day of shared writing, I help the class plan a very simple story, with a clear beginning, middle, and end about the character we created. I explain that often the character and the problem are introduced in the beginning, the character often tries to solve the problem in the middle, and the problem is usually solved by the end. We use yesterday's work to plan how each of these parts will go—one page at a time. I touch three pieces of chart paper—one for the beginning, middle, and end—as we quickly decide what we will write on each page. Then I sketch our plan at the top of each page before we move to drafting.

Figure 3.2

As we draft, I often prompt the class to consider a few qualities of good writing. Perhaps I'll mention that stories often start with a character doing or saying something, and then ask the class how our first sentence might go. I might remind students that authors usually let us know how characters are feeling, and I then ask them how our character might be feeling in the beginning of our story. At the very least, I make sure we stick to our plan and that we write a cohesive, realistic story that lets our readers know about a character that faces a problem, which ultimately gets solved.

I want everyone to participate during shared writing, but I also want to make quick decisions about what to write on the page, so we can honor our short timeframe. So each time I prompt the class, I move between asking students to share their ideas with the person sitting next to them, and calling on individual partners (usually those whose ideas I have heard while circulating) to direct me in what I should write on the page. (See Figure 3.3 for an example of a shared story. I doubt I would have been able to come up with a more creative plotline than this class of six year olds!)

Bob is 10 years old and he is sad because he doesn't like his name. He doesn't like bs and he has two in his name. And, he wants a long name with 10 letters instead of a short name with three!

Bob asks his dad, "Can I change my name?" His dad says, "No!" Bob feels angry and disappointed.

Bob says to his mom, "Dad won't let me change my name and I'm disappointed and mad!"

His mom says, "It's okay, honey. I'll call you Christopher." Bob feels happy!

Figure 3.3

Using Published Texts to Support Our Shared Writing of a Realistic Story

We want to select one published text to use during shared writing. Ideally, we would use one of the mentor texts we plan to rely on most heavily for the duration of the unit. Before we ask students during shared writing to think about the characters, problem, and solution in our mentor text, we will want to do that work ourselves, as I do below, to make sure we can scaffold student thinking in appropriate ways. We won't share this work with students, but it will help us support them better when they encounter difficulty. For example, if we ask our class to recall inside traits of a published character and they respond with outside traits, or with nothing at all, we will be better equipped to help them find examples of inside traits in our mentor text if we have already done the work ourselves. If you want help finding an appropriate text, you might refer to Chapter 1 where I address criteria for choosing mentor texts and suggest a few options by grade level.

The Carrot Seed, Ruth Krauss

Character sketch:

The little boy's outside traits	The little boy's inside traits
Young, about five to seven years old	Doesn't give up
Has a mother, father, and big brother	Responsible (takes good care of his carrot seed)
Short, curly hair	Likes gardening
Wears overalls and a hat	Patient

Problem: He plants a carrot seed and everyone in his family says it won't come up.

Solution: He nonetheless takes good care of his seed, watering and weeding, and one day a carrot does come up.

Goggles!, Ezra Jack Keats

Character sketch:

Peter's outside traits	Peter's inside traits
Boy	Brave (stands up to the big boys)
About eight years old	Smart (tricks the big boys)
Brown skin	Close with his dog and his friend, Archie
Short, dark, curly hair	Generous (shares his goggles with Archie)
Wears black pants and a red T-shirt	Good friend
Has a special hideout	

Problem: Some older boys try to steal the goggles that Peter found.

Solution: Peter's dog, Willie, snatches the goggles before the older boys can take them. Willie runs away and soon meets Peter at his hideout with the goggles.

Big Sister and Little Sister, Charlotte Zolotow

Character sketch:

Little sister's outside traits	Little sister's inside traits
Girl	Very close with big sister
About four to eight years old	Sometimes likes to be alone
Straight, blonde hair	Usually listens to big sister, but not always
Wears pigtails	Can be independent
Wears dresses	Brave (leaves home alone)
Has big sister	Caring and gentle
Lives in a big house in the country	

In many stories for this age, there is an obvious, central character. However, this book feels equally about big sister and little sister. The class can simply vote on the one they want to focus on for this character work.

Problem: Little sister is tired of big sister telling her what to do, so she runs away to be alone. Big sister can't find her, and she cries.

Solution: Little sister takes care of big sister—just like she's learned to do from big sister taking care of her.

Assessing Students' Understanding During Shared Writing

We will informally assess students' general understandings of realistic fiction and the process of crafting a story by listening to their conversations and contributions during shared writing. The questions below can guide our assessment. If students are struggling, you may want to reference one of the corresponding sections on assessment in an upcoming chapter for ways to provide additional support:

:: Do students understand what makes a character realistic? Can they generate inside and outside character traits? (If not, see ideas in the section on assessment on page 45–46.)

:: Can students generate believable problems? (If not, see the section on assessment on page 50.)

:: Can students generate believable solutions that correspond with those problems? (If not, see the section on assessment on page 54.)

:: Can students plan a focused, realistic story with a clear beginning, middle, and end? If not, see the section on assessment on pages 60–61.)

CHAPTER 4

Generating Topics and Planning

As excited as our students may be to craft their own realistic fiction, I know as a teacher and as a writer that figuring out what to write about and exactly how to begin are among the most daunting stages of the writing process. Even now, as I attempt to begin a new chapter, the blank page intimidates me. Where should I begin? What is it, exactly, that I want to say? Toward the beginning of any genre unit, my main goal is to give students the tools they need to address these potentially overwhelming questions and concerns. I want to make sure they are energized—not paralyzed—as we dig into our exciting work at hand.

Overview

This stage of the unit will likely last five to seven days. I have four primary goals; before I move the class to the next stage, I want students to understand how to:

1. Create and develop their own realistic characters to get them ready to write stories in which characters are as important as plot.
2. Generate a list of realistic problems their characters might face.
3. Generate different ways a problem might be solved realistically.
4. Plan how their stories will go before they draft.

I describe each goal below and offer strategies you might use to help students internalize understandings. Though there will not be time to cover everything during whole-class mini-lessons, you might find some of the following teaching topics appropriate for differentiated instruction and for middle- and end-of-the-workshop teaching.

I. Creating Characters

When I teach young students to write realistic fiction, I focus on three critical features of the genre: character, problem, and solution. (As we teach these features, we can refer back to the shared story we wrote toward the beginning of the unit to help students better understand the work we want them to do independently.)

Possible Mini-Lessons to Help Students Create Characters

Choose 2–3 mini-lessons from below.

One of the reasons I love teaching students to write fiction is because I have always fantasized about writing fiction myself. Sometimes, I start stories in my head, or I write stories with my five-year-old son, Harrison. When I'm feeling extremely bold, I may jot ideas in a notebook. Through my experimentation with fiction, I have come to learn that there are many different ways to begin. At times, my thinking begins with plot. Occasionally, it takes shape around a particular setting. But most often, my stories emerge from the creation of a character. I think different writers tend to gravitate toward different starting points, and you may experiment with different ways to begin in your classroom. I like to begin by teaching students to create and develop characters, just as many published authors do when they write fiction (Bernays and Painter, 1995; Peck, 1983). Before we teach the next steps to writing fiction, students should follow this simple sequence: name a character, develop it, then create at least one more so they have some choice when the time comes to settle on a character. Especially in kindergarten, students will develop characters through drawing as well as writing. For example, they might add color details to show their character's hair, skin, and eye color, and they might draw objects or pets to show what is important to their character. See Figures 4.1–4.3 for characters created by kindergarten through second grade writers.

Figure 4.1—Daisy's character chart, Kindergarten

Dandelion

Outside traits	Inside traits
She has blond hair.	She is nice.
She smiles.	She is afraid of what's at night.
She wears red.	
She has blue eyes.	
She is five years old.	
She wears brown.	

Max

Outside traits	Inside traits
5 years old.	He is almost too helpful!
He has brown hair.	He has a garden.
His mom is Chinese.	He likes to play outside.
He is a boy.	
He has a mom and a dad.	

Rachel

Outside traits	Inside traits
She is a girl.	Her favorite color is purple.
She has brown eyes.	She likes to jump rope.
She has long, dark, and curly hair.	She loves herself.
She almost always wears dresses every day.	
She has two moms.	
She is 8 years old.	

Molly

Outside traits	Inside traits
Girl	Wants a dog
9 years old	Likes to draw
Right size for her age	Loves to go places
Speaks English	Nice
Likes to plan clothing	Hates bullies
Not in a rush	Loves to play hide-and-go-seek in the night
	Collects buttons

Figure 4.2a—Linnea's first character chart, first grade

Figure 4.2b—Linnea's second character chart, first grade

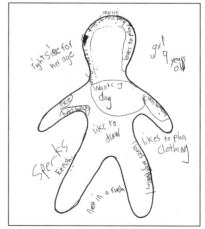

Figure 4.3—Leah's character chart, second grade

Brainstorm outside character details

Once we explain that outside details are anything we know about a person simply by looking at them, it helps to name different types of outside details, so students think beyond what a character is wearing and what color hair she has. We could create a chart, "Ways to Develop Characters," and ask students to help us brainstorm other traits. A typical list might include some or all of the following:

- :: Name
- :: Gender and age
- :: Dress
- :: Size and shape
- :: Color: hair, skin, eyes
- :: Body movements
- :: Facial expressions
- :: Speech: language, voice, volume
- :: Family members
- :: Home location and type
- :: School and grade

After we teach our first mini-lesson on creating characters, students will return to their seats and start working on their own characters. When working in the primary grades, I teach students to quickly draw the outline of a person and to record outside traits in the margins; again, especially in kindergarten classrooms, we can also teach students to draw outside traits. In case you prefer to supply the graphic organizer for your students' character charts, I include one in the appendix.

Brainstorm inside character details

Like us, characters "are more than descriptions, body language, and dialogue" (Bernays and Painter, 1995, 53). Inside details are what we learn about a character as we get to know him or her. They are also the details that make for character- versus plot-driven stories, and hence, they are the details that bring meaning to a story. Though external events are certainly important, what ultimately matters is how characters respond to those events. I could write two stories about the same event: one in which a girl slips in the hall and laughs because she thinks it is so funny, and another in which a girl slips and weeps with humiliation. The meaning of each of those stories is fundamentally different and is determined by the character and what kind of person she is on the *inside*.

Though it is often more automatic for students to develop outside details because they are more tangible, we can help make inside details tangible as well by naming them. Doing so helps even the youngest writers create more dynamic characters who come to life on the page. A typical class might brainstorm a list that includes some or all of the following:

:: Fears

:: Wants

:: Typical feelings

:: Strengths

:: Problems

:: Important relationships

:: Treatment of others

:: Favorite things to do and favorite places

Once we teach students about inside traits, we can teach them to record them on the inside of their character outlines. However, students often confuse inside and outside traits, as shown when they write things like "long hair" on the inside of their characters and "lonely" on the outside. What's most important for our youngest writers is that they generate inside and outside traits, not necessarily that they can always identify the difference between the two.

Use people we know for inspiration

If students are struggling to create characters or to describe those characters, we might teach them to turn to their own lives for ideas. Because young writers sometimes mistakenly write true stories instead of fiction, we can teach them to borrow traits from several different people when developing a single character. They might first think about a close friend and consider what stands out that could also be true about their character. Then they might think about a parent, a neighbor, a cousin, or a teacher. When I model this work for students, I emphasize how I hone in on *unique* traits: that my best friend sticks her feet out of the covers when she sleeps and doesn't like the different foods on her plate to touch; that my husband leaves a trail of socks and spare change wherever he goes; that my son never stops moving, even stands and sways from side to side when he eats dinner. We can also model how to return to our chart, "Ways to Develop Characters," to make sure we are generating a range of traits, both internal and external. I model thinking like: "I describe a lot of things from this side of the chart, on external traits—what my character wears, how old she is, who she lives with—but I don't describe a lot of things from this side of the chart, on internal traits. Let's see . . . I see 'fears' on this chart, but I didn't write about my character's fears. Let me think . . . What fears do people in my life have? I know, my daughter is a little afraid of loud noises; she always clings to my legs when a plane or large truck zooms by. Maybe my character could feel and act the same way."

Create unique and specific qualities

Whether or not students are getting inspiration from people in their lives, we can encourage them to generate unique character details—those aspects that will make their characters more memorable. We can also encourage them to balance general descriptors (like "responsible" and "has a big family") with specific details (like "always does his homework and takes really good care of his little sister" and "has four older sisters, a younger brother and eleven cousins"). Being more specific helps bring characters to life. It allows students to get to know their characters well, and it makes it much more likely that readers will also get the chance to know them well. If your students are limited by their ability to generate a lot of writing, teach them to sketch important details, when possible, and potentially label them; for example, they might draw several stick figures and write "family" next to them.

Using Published Texts to Teach Students How to Create Realistic Characters

If we have already used shared writing to sketch a character from a published text, we can refer to that work as we teach students how to create their own characters. If we did not do the shared writing described in Chapter 3, we might now look for a published story in which we get to know a variety of inside and outside details about a character; using a list of different ways to describe characters can help us pull from our published text an assortment of traits. We might chart them in groups of inside and outside traits to help students grasp the difference. We might also name for students what aspect of the character each trait describes to help them understand the range of things they, too, could describe about their characters. For example:

Knuffle Bunny Too, Mo Willems

Trixie's outside traits	Trixie's inside traits
Girl (Gender)	Gets excited to do new things (Feelings and actions)
Five or six years old (Age)	Best friend is Sonja (Relationships)
Straight, blond hair (Looks; hair color)	Loves her stuffed animal Knuffle Bunny (Likes)
Light skin (Skin color)	Strong-willed; knows what she wants (Strengths)
Has a mom and a dad (Family)	Talks a lot (Acts)
Lives in Brooklyn (Lives)	
Speaks English (Language)	

My Friend and I, Lisa Jahn-Clough

Girl's outside traits	Girl's inside traits
Girl (Gender)	Likes to sing and dance (Favorite things to do)
Around five to ten (Age)	Likes to play (Favorite things to do)
Has long, brown hair (Looks; hair color)	Good at making friends (Strengths)
Wears pigtails (Looks)	Sometimes grabs (Problems)
Brown skin (Skin color)	Helpful—helps fix the bunny (Strengths)
Wears purple a lot (Wears)	Has strong feelings—feels lonely, angry, sad, relieved, joyful (Feelings)
Lives in a house (Lives)	Very close to friend next door (Important relationships)
Lives next door to friend (Lives)	

Sheila Rae the Brave, Kevin Henkes

Sheila Rae's Outside Traits and What They Describe	Sheila Rae's Inside Traits and What They Describe
A mouse in the pictures but could be an ordinary girl (Looks)	Brave (Strengths)
Maybe eight to twelve years old (Age)	Afraid of being lost (Fears)
Has a mother, father, and little sister (Family members)	Imaginative (Strengths)
Wears dresses a lot (Wears)	Active—likes riding bikes and playing jump rope (Acts; Favorite things to do)
Lives in a house (Lives)	Close with sister (Important relationships)
Lives close to school—walks there (Lives)	

Remember that when we use books like Henkes' in which the characters are realistic except for the fact that pictures depict them as animals, we need to remind students to look beyond the pictures. They should imagine the characters as people and understand that in true realistic fiction, animals do not talk. If we expect a certain group of students will be unable to look beyond the pictures, we should choose a different mentor text.

Preparing Our Own Writing to Teach Students How to Create Realistic Characters

Try this: Create and develop two different characters, one male and one female, with a variety of inside and outside traits. Make sure you include at least two wants and two fears for each, since you will need to know those later in the unit. As always, think about your students' writing level, and aim to create something slightly above what the majority of your class could do independently (see Figure 4.4 for one of my character webs in which I generate a range of internal and external traits for Zoe).

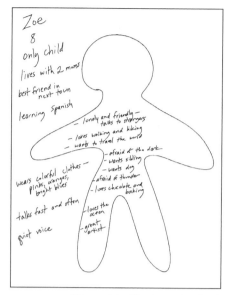

Figure 4.4—My character chart

Assessing Students' Understanding of How to Create Realistic Characters

As a general rule, I encourage teachers to collect writing folders weekly and spend no more than 90 minutes (or we won't have time to do it weekly), quickly assessing students' current understandings. Doing so allows us to plan or revise our lessons for the following week based on the pressing needs of the majority of our students. It also allows us to group students for differentiated instruction based on shared needs and to begin to think about individual conferences we might have.

One way to help make these assessments quick is to generate a weekly list of four to six qualities (including at least one convention skill) we want to look for in our students' writing; we can use them as lenses to focus our assessment so the task becomes less time-consuming, less overwhelming, and more directly linked to the teaching we need to do for a more successful unit. (See the appendix for a blank assessment chart. If you write your students' names on the chart at the beginning of the year, you can easily make copies and simply add what you want to assess each week.) When it comes time to collect students' work, you might include on your list of lenses one or more of the following to assess their understanding of this stage of the unit: realistic characters; inside traits; outside traits. You might spend three or four minutes with each writing folder, skimming the character charts each student developed, and checking off on your assessment chart what the student seems to understand.

As always, in addition to collecting writing folders weekly, we will informally assess students' understandings when they share their thinking during whole-class mini-lessons as we circulate the room during independent writing and when we confer with individuals and small groups. Whether engaging in more formal or informal assessment, the following assessment question and corresponding supports can help guide our thinking and teaching:

Can students create make-believe yet believable characters and develop them with inside and outside traits?

:: If characters are real people, help students fictionalize them by adding new traits that do not belong to the person they are describing. For example, if they are describing themselves or a best friend, you might help them include traits from several other people in their lives as well.

:: If characters are not realistic, students can borrow traits from people in their lives to make them more believable.

:: If characters are not realistic, teach students to ask themselves, "Could this be true in real life?" as they re-read each trait.

II. Generating Realistic Problems

Though I generally teach students to begin realistic fiction by creating characters, other teachers (and authors) begin by imagining possible problems. However *you* begin, teach students to connect these critical elements, so that it makes sense for their characters to face the problems they do.

Possible Mini-Lessons to Help Students Generate Problems

I think of characters as the heart and soul of a story, and problems and solutions as the skeleton; in more technical terms, the problem and solution make the plot. One of my primary goals is to teach students how to generate focused, meaningful plots. That work begins by generating believable problems, the types of everyday challenges that happen to people just like our students and to which they and their readers can relate.

Because I always want to maximize students' choice as writers, I encourage them to generate multiple possibilities before settling on the one they want to pursue. This means choosing a character (they might repeat this work later with additional characters) and brainstorming at least two or three problems that character might face. In doing so, students begin to envision how different stories could take shape, and they begin to internalize the importance of problems in the stories they read and write. (See Figure 4.5 for an example of student work from this step of the unit; see the appendix for graphic organizers students might use as they think about problems and eventually solutions.)

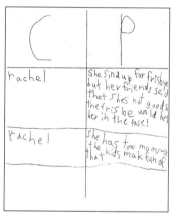

Figure 4.5—Linnea's list of possible problems, first grade

C [Characters]	P [Problems]
Rachel	She signs up for Frisbee but her friends said that she's not good, so the Frisbee would hit her in the face!
Rachel	She has two moms and the kids make fun of that.

Consider what problems might arise from a character's wants and fears

Though we teach character development in this unit to lay the foundation for eventually writing character-driven stories, the reality is that most of our youngest writers will write plot-driven stories: stories that we hope include rich information about characters, but ones that are ultimately about a problem and its solution. One way to honor the importance of characters while teaching toward plot is to maintain the link between these two story elements. If most of our students successfully brainstormed wants and fears when they developed their characters, I recommend teaching them to use those wants and fears as a springboard for possible problems. For example, when I look at my character chart for Zoe, I see that she wants a sibling, wants a dog, is afraid of the dark, and is afraid of thunder. "Since Zoe wants a sibling," I might say to students, "perhaps one problem could be that her parents don't want any more kids. Or another problem could be that what Zoe really wants is a little sister, but she is about to get a little brother—that could definitely feel like a problem for Zoe! Hmmm . . . what's a totally different problem Zoe might have? Let me look again at her wants and fears. I see she's afraid of the dark. I wonder what problems that might cause? I know my son is afraid of the dark and it's mostly a problem at night because he often has a hard time falling asleep on his own. Maybe Zoe could have a similar problem: maybe she's really tired and cranky all the time, because she gets so scared at night that she can't fall asleep. I wonder what other problems her fear might cause?"

Once I model for students, they can practice themselves by helping me brainstorm additional problems: "Zoe also wants a dog and is also afraid of thunder. Would you help me think of some other problems her wants and fears might cause?"

Consider problems in your life, in the lives of people around you, and in the lives of other characters you know

If students need more support brainstorming problems, or if they have not successfully brainstormed their characters' wants and fears, we can teach them to think of problems in isolation rather than in connection with their characters. Because we are teaching realistic fiction, we continually want to emphasize the need to create everyday, believable story elements. We can teach students to do what so many writers in the world do: draw inspiration from our own experiences and from those around us.

When we teach students to draw inspiration from everyday life, we'll also want to remind them that they are writing fiction and hence need to change details so as not to write fact. For example, if one of my problems over the weekend is that I fell off my bike and scraped my knees, perhaps my character could fall off a swing and hurt his wrist. Similarly, if a problem in a favorite book of mine is that the character's cat runs away, perhaps my character could lose a hamster; or perhaps she wants a cat but can't have one. Again, instead of inadvertently teaching students to retell what they have done, seen, or read, we want to model how one idea can lead to a variety of fresh ideas.

Consider everything you know about your character and imagine what problems she might face

Another way to help students maintain the connection between their characters and the problems they face is to show them how to move back and forth between their character charts and their list of problems. Though focusing on wants and fears is a more concrete approach, other details can just as effectively lead to challenges. For example, the fact that my character Zoe is a great artist could yield a list of problems: perhaps she needs new art supplies but can't afford them; maybe she wants to take an art class but there is no more room for her; maybe she spills paint all over her rug and worries about getting into trouble.

Using Published Texts to Teach Students to Generate Realistic Problems

Though we are not yet teaching students to generate solutions, we will very soon, and I recommend using the same text to teach both problem and solution. To make our teaching as clear as possible, we want to choose texts in which we can easily pinpoint a central problem and corresponding solution; since our students will be creating stories with a similarly straightforward structure, we won't want to use mentor stories with a series of interwoven problems and solutions. Finally, we will want to reference multiple problems and solutions,which means gathering two to four published texts that can be used for this part of the unit on problems as well as the next part on solutions. All of the books I recommend in Chapter 1 provide excellent examples, including the following:

Julius's Candy Corn, Kevin Henkes

Problem: Julius wants to eat the cupcakes his mom made, but his mom tells him to wait for the party.

The Stray Dog, Marc Simont

Problem: The family finds a stray dog that it wants to take home. But a dogcatcher says he is going to take the dog to the pound because he doesn't have a collar or leash, which proves he doesn't belong to anyone.

Melissa Parkington's Beautiful, Beautiful Hair, Pat Brisson

Problem: Melissa wants to be noticed for something she does, not simply for her beautiful hair.

Preparing Our Own Writing to Teach Students to Generate Realistic Problems

Try this: Using your character chart, choose one want and list at least two problems it might cause; do the same for one fear. Now pick an outside detail and again brainstorm two or three problems it might cause. For example, because my character Zoe wants a dog, I generated the following problems: Zoe wants a dog, but her parents say no; Zoe wants a dog, but she is allergic; Zoe wants a dog, but she is not allowed to have dogs in her apartment. Based on Zoe's fear of thunderstorms, she might face the following problems: She never wants to leave the house when it is raining; kids at school tease her for hiding under the desk when it thunders. Finally, in looking at the outside details on my chart, I picked, "Zoe has two moms" and generated the following problems: A kid at school teases Zoe because she has two moms; Zoe's school is having a father-daughter dance and she feels left out because she doesn't have a father.

Assessing Students' Understanding of Realistic Problems

We will continue to assess students' understandings as they work with us and with their peers during writing workshop. When we collect their writing folders at the end of the week, we might include "realistic problems" on our list of lenses. The question and corresponding supports below can help guide our assessment and follow-up teaching of realistic problems.

Can students generate a variety of fictional yet believable problems?

:: If students struggle to generate problems, give them a stack of short, familiar texts and show them how to list the problems in each text. Then teach them how to change the specifics slightly to come up with new problems.

:: Students might talk with friends and family about some of the problems they have in a day and make a list. During writing, they could use their list as inspiration for the types of problems their characters might face.

:: If students are listing problems exactly like ones they have experienced (in other words, writing fact instead of fiction), teach them to use a topic but change the details. For example, if they had a fight with a friend, they could use the topic "fighting" and perhaps have their character fight with a sibling or parent; or if they really want a new toy, they might use the topic of wanting something and have their character want a new book or game.

:: If the problems do not seem realistic, tell students to ask themselves, "Could this *really* happen in real life? Have I ever known or heard about something like this actually occurring?"

:: If students can only generate one problem, teach another strategy from the lesson ideas above and have them use it to brainstorm a new problem. Or, teach students to consider each character trait, one by one, and what problem(s) it might cause.

III. Generating Realistic Solutions

At this point in the unit, we hope students will have at least two character sketches and at least two possible problems for one of those characters. Of course, some students will have much more writing than this, anything from several characters to a long list of possible problems, maybe even a drafted story.

Possible Mini-Lessons to Help Students Generate Solutions

Choose 1–2 mini-lessons from the list below.

When we teach students to generate solutions, we can remind them that this is the third critical story element in realistic fiction. (See Figure 4.6 for an example of student-generated problems and solutions.)

Problems	Solutions
Her problem is she wants to live in the country.	She moves to the country.
	She went to different places that were like the country.
She is afraid of spooky noises at night.	She wore ear-muffs.

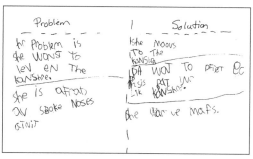

Figure 4.6—Daisy's list of problems and solutions, kindergarten

Consider everyday solutions for the problems characters face— the types of solutions we see around us

By this part of the unit, most students have likely grasped the concept of *realistic* fiction. This means we can teach them to think about everyday solutions to their problems and trust that most will stay away from aliens saving the day or fairy godmothers arriving with magic wands. However, a more subtle challenge often emerges, one that yields solutions that are not *entirely* realistic: parents that easily grant children new siblings when they ask or bullies who suddenly and inexplicably act with compassion. I think the issue is that students are often more focused on what they want for their characters, and maybe even focused on how they wish people in the world would act, rather than on what is truly believable. We might celebrate the fact that our students are embracing the power of words—the ability to use writing to envision and maybe even encourage new possibilities in life.

Of course, we also want to teach toward a deeper understanding of the genre and what it means to use writing to reflect truth. So first, we can teach students to think about real-life solutions by looking to the world around us and noticing how people overcome challenging situations. Then, we might teach students to reflect on those solutions with questions like, "Would my [parent, sibling, friend, teacher, and so on] say or do something like this? Is this *really* how things happen in the world?" As with everything, students will internalize varying degrees of understanding, and in many cases, we will allow for the uncharacteristically appeasing mother—as long as she isn't sprouting wings to fly to the rescue!

Consider different ways to solve a problem: the character might solve it herself or someone else might solve it for her

Especially if students struggle to brainstorm multiple solutions for the same problem, we can teach them about different ways to overcome a challenge. Teaching students to imagine what different characters could do gives them very concrete strategies for generating solutions. In some cases, they may introduce a new character to bring forth a resolution; in other cases, they can simply think about the characters that already exist in their stories and different options each one has to solve the problem at hand.

Think about the message we want to send to readers about how people in the world can or should behave

More sophisticated writers and thinkers may be ready to learn in explicit terms about the power we have as writers to influence people's thinking. Realistic fiction is not merely a reflection of the world around us; it is also a tool for impacting that world. We can teach students that the way characters solve problems in stories sends a message to readers about how we might solve problems in our own lives. Let's imagine a story in which a character is teased at school and consider the significance of different solutions. If the victim tells a teacher what is happening and the teacher steps in to stop the bullying, it might encourage readers to turn to adults for help. If a bystander intervenes in the victim's defense, it might encourage readers to help when they see others in trouble. If the victim stands up for herself and successfully stops the bullying, it might encourage readers to face their tormentors. When we encourage students to consider the types of behaviors they would like to see in their own communities, they begin to grasp the power they have as writers to affect those communities.

Using Published Texts to Teach Students How to Generate Realistic Solutions

We want to use the same texts to model problems and solutions. (For more details, see the earlier section on using published texts to teach problems.) When it comes time to teach solutions, we will want to remind students of the problem in each story, so they can connect it with the corresponding solution, as I do below:

Julius's Candy Corn, Kevin Henkes

Problem: Julius wants to eat the cupcakes his mom made, but his mom tells him to wait for the party.

Solution: Julius eats the candy corn on top of the cupcakes instead.

The Stray Dog, Marc Simont

Problem: The family finds a stray dog that it wants to take home. But a dogcatcher says he is going to take the dog to the pound because he doesn't have a collar or leash, which proves he doesn't belong to anyone.

Solution: The boy takes off his belt and says it is the dog's collar, the girl takes off her hair ribbon and says it is the dog's leash, and they tell the dogcatcher that the dog belongs to them.

Melissa Parkington's Beautiful, Beautiful Hair, Pat Brisson

Problem: Melissa wants to be noticed for something she does, not simply for her beautiful hair.

Solution: Melissa decides to be the kindest person in the whole town since someone has to *do* something to be kind. She starts helping a lot of people, and eventually she cuts off her hair to donate to kids who need wigs.

Preparing Our Own Writing to Teach Students How to Generate Realistic Solutions

Try this: Choose one of the problems your character could face and think about ways you've seen this problem solved in books you've read and/or in the lives of people around you. List two to three possible solutions. Now choose another problem and think about different messages you could send readers through the solution; make at least one of those solutions arise through your character's actions and at least one from someone who intervenes. For example, one problem on my list is that Zoe wants a dog but her parents say "no." In *Henry and Mudge*, Henry first wants a sibling and a new house, but his parents say no. So when he finally asks for a dog, they say yes. Perhaps my character could ask for (and get) something other than a dog—like a fish. Similarly, I've known people who wanted dogs or horses and couldn't have them, so they found other ways to be with those animals, either through volunteering or spending time with friends' pets. Perhaps Zoe could become a dog walker, or maybe she could spend more time with her neighbor's dog.

Another problem on my list is that a kid makes fun of Zoe because she has two mothers. If Zoe were the one to solve that problem, it could be by standing up to the bully, saying something about how lucky she is to have two parents that love her. If someone else were to solve the problem, it could be a teacher who overhears the teasing and puts a stop to it.

Assessing Students' Understanding of Realistic Solutions

We will continue to informally assess students' understandings during writing workshop. When we collect their writing folders at the end of the week, we might include "realistic solutions" on our list of lenses. The following question and corresponding supports can help guide our assessment and follow-up teaching of solutions.

Can students generate a variety of fictional yet believable solutions?

:: Teach students to list the solutions in a stack of familiar texts and to use them as inspiration for their own solutions.

:: Teach students to think about the outcome they want for their stories and to consider what might happen to produce that outcome.

:: Teach students to list a few different people from different *groups* (friends, family, teachers, and so on) in their character's life and then imagine what each person might do to help solve the problem.

:: Teach students to ask themselves questions such as, "Would this *really* happen like this? Have I ever known people like this character to act this way in real life?"

IV. Planning Our Stories

For each story students write, they need to choose a character, and then choose from their lists of problems and solutions which ones will drive the plot. I usually teach students to choose one problem and one solution. More sophisticated writers might incorporate multiple problems and/or solutions into a single story *if* they connect and can be strung together without losing focus. For example, I could write about my character Zoe in a story with one problem and solution: She really wants a dog; she asks her parents, but they say no, so she gets a fish instead. Or, I could write the story with a series of problems and attempted solutions followed by the ultimate resolution: Zoe is lonely and asks for a sibling; when her parents say no, she asks for a dog instead; when they say no again, she gets a job as a dog walker; she asks for a fish, to which her parents finally say yes.

What I *don't* want students to plan and write are stories about a series of events in which the ultimate solution is disconnected from the initial problem. Imagine the following: a girl whose parents say no to a dog, so they get into a fight and the girl gets into trouble; because she's grounded she misses her friend's birthday party and her friend gets mad; she and her friend fight, and the girl makes a new friend. Even though one event leads to the next, and even though the story includes a problem and a solution, the overall story lacks focus and hence meaning, leaving us to wonder, "What is this piece *really* about?"

Mini-Lessons to Help Students Plan Their Stories

Choose one mini-lesson from the list below.

Once students have a character, problem, and solution, they have essentially planned their stories. Still, to help them maintain their focus as they draft, we usually want to teach a reminder lesson on a way to plan exactly how those stories will unfold. (Remember, some students will have already jumped into drafting; they will naturally gravitate in that direction if they complete the previous steps of the unit before other students. The difference is that we are now teaching them how to do that work even better, which they can now practice with a new story.) Before we teach any of the following lessons, we need to decide whether we want students to plan stories with three or four parts; in kindergarten, I recommend three-part plans with a very concrete beginning, middle, and end. By second grade, we might teach four-part plans that have two middle scenes; or we might give students the option to choose for themselves.

Touch a separate page for each part and say what you will write in the beginning, middle, and end; then sketch your plan for each page

To prepare for this lesson, we need to create blank booklets for the class. Depending on the number of parts we want students to plan for, we can staple together three or four pieces of paper; students can always add additional pages if they like. (In the next chapter on drafting, I explain the reasons for encouraging young writers to compose each part on a different page.) In our lesson, we can teach students how to plan by touching each page of their blank book, saying to themselves what they plan to write where, and then quickly sketching each of those parts on the appropriate page.

As we model, we can also show students how planning helps us catch and rethink problem areas before we put them in writing. "Watch how I plan my story about Zoe," I might say to the class. "On this first page, I'm going to write how Zoe wants a dog but her mom says no; and on this second page I'm going to write how she gets a fish instead . . . Uh-oh, that's actually my whole story, but if I put it all on the first two pages, what am I going to put on this last page? It all ended so quickly! I really want to stretch my story out across at least three pages, so there is a clear beginning, middle, and end for my readers."

"I better rethink things; let me try again. Maybe in the beginning, I could write about how Zoe wants a dog but her mom says no. Now let me think, I don't want to end it yet, so before she solves the problem, what else could Zoe do? I know, maybe she could try to solve her problem, just like the characters do in the books we've been reading. If I were a kid and wanted something, and one parent said no, what might I do? Well, I might be sneaky and try asking another parent. Remember, my character Zoe has two moms, so maybe she could ask her other mom for a dog! I like that, I'm going to write that on this middle page here. And then in the end, on this page, I'll show Zoe asking for a fish instead and her parents finally saying yes. Now I need to go back and sketch each of those parts before I start writing, so I'm sure to remember what I want to happen on every page."

Use a story map to plan the beginning, middle, and end of the story

If we think students would benefit from a written plan, we can teach them how to quickly jot each part of their stories on a story map or timeline. Because there are many ways for the plot to unfold across the beginning, middle, and end of a story, we might show students a couple of different options. The choices might include length—a three-part plan or a four-part plan. They might also include different ways to focus each part. For example, students might introduce the character in the beginning, show the problem in the middle, and show the solution at the end. Alternatively, they might introduce the problem in the beginning, show the character *trying* to solve it in the middle, and show the ultimate solution at the end. (See the sections on using published texts and using our own writing for examples.) Most students will develop one plan, but some might generate a few possibilities before choosing the one they like best. (See Figure 4.7 for a student's story map as well as the piece he ultimately published. See the appendix for different graphic organizers students might use to plan their stories.)

Beginning	Middle	End
Katelyn says she is not scared of anything.	One night there is a thunderstorm.	She goes upstairs and asks her brother, "Will you play with me?"

Figure 4.7a—Plan and draft by Jacob, second grade

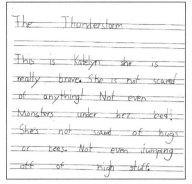

One thing she is scared of thunderstorms. She doesn't tell anyone because shes embarrassed.

Figure 4.7b—Plan and draft by Jacob, second grade

The Thunderstorm

This is Katelyn. She is really brave. She is not scared of anything! Not even monsters under her bed! She's not scared of bugs or bees. Not even jumping off high stuff.

One thing she is scared of is thunderstorms. She doesn't tell anyone because she's embarrassed.

One night it was raining and she heard Chhhhhh Chhhhhh.

She ran upstairs and screamed. She went into her brother's room.

She shook her brother and said "Wake up." Her brother said . . . "What, who is it, oh, it's you Katelyn. What do you want?"

"Will you play with me?" she said. Katelyn's brother said "yes." So now she's not scared anymore.

Tell your story to a writing partner, making sure to stay focused on the problem and solution; then sketch each part of your story across the pages

Rehearsing how a story will go is another excellent way to plan. We might teach students to simply tell the bare bones of their stories: a sentence or two about what happens first, next, and at the end. Or we could use this as an opportunity to revisit the qualities of strong oral stories by teaching students to tell their stories to a writing partner exactly as they will appear on paper, including things like character feelings and words— or whatever strategies students have already learned for crafting strong stories.

Because it will take most students multiple days to draft their stories, many will easily forget the exact sequence of events they told their partners. As with the first strategy on planning, we can teach students to sketch the beginning, middle, and end across pages after they tell their stories and before they put words on the page.

Using Published Texts to Teach Students How to Plan

If we use published texts to teach our students how to plan, it may look and feel different than usual. Even when we can find published examples of the thinking and planning authors did before sitting down to draft a story, those plans tend to be much more complicated than the ones we will teach our kindergarten, first, and second grade students to create, and so we may not want to use them as mentor texts. We could, however, create an *imagined* plan for a published story, as I do below. For most stories, we can imagine a three-part or a four-part plan (or an even longer plan, though it is unlikely we would teach K–2 students to plan for more than four parts). In the following examples, I put what could be the fourth part of each story inside brackets.

Lilly's Chocolate Heart, Kevin Henkes

Based on what we know about the story, Henkes likely planned to introduce the problem in the beginning, show the character trying to solve it in the middle [then show the character trying to solve it again], and show the ultimate solution at the end: In the beginning, Lilly wants to find the perfect hiding place for her last piece of Valentine's candy. In the middle, Lilly looks for a hiding place. [Then she looks in more and more places.] At the end, Lilly finds the perfect hiding place—her mouth!

Bailey Goes Camping, Kevin Henkes

Henkes probably planned to introduce the problem in the beginning, show the problem in the middle [then show the character *trying* to solve the problem], and show the solution at the end: In the beginning, we learn that Bruce and Betty are going camping, but their little brother Bailey has to stay home. In the middle, Bruce and Betty talk about all the great things they're going to do while camping, and explain that Bailey can go, too, when he's older; Bailey says it's not fair. [Bailey's parents keep trying to get Bailey to do something else fun with them, like play ball or bake cookies.] At the end, Bailey's mom says they can do the fun camping activities Bruce and Betty talked about right in their house, so they do things like set up a tent in the living room.

Ish, Peter H. Reynolds

Based on what we know about the story, Reynolds likely planned to introduce important character details in the beginning, show the problem in the middle, [then show the character *trying* to solve the problem], and show the solution at the end. In the beginning, we learn that Ramon loves to draw. In the middle, his brother makes fun of his art, which makes Ramon crumple up all the drawings he makes. [Or: First his brother makes fun of his art. Then Ramon tries and tries to draw things "right" before giving up.] At the end of the story, Ramon finds his crumpled art hung all over his sister's walls, which makes him feel better about his art, and so he starts to draw again.

Preparing Our Own Writing to Teach Students How to Plan

Try this: If you have not already done so, choose one of your characters, one of the problems she or he might face, and one of the corresponding solutions. Now use the graphic organizer below (see the appendix for a reproducible) to plan how your story will unfold:

Beginning (*Introduce character and/or problem*)	**Middle** (*Show problem or show character* trying *to solve the problem*)	**End** (*Show solution*)

If you think your students are ready to write more complex, four-part stories, use the following to plan your story:

Beginning (*Introduce character and/or problem*)	**Middle** (*Show problem*)	**Middle** (*Show problem happening again or show a character* trying *to solve the problem*)	**End** (*Show solution*)

Below are two ways my story could go.

Beginning (*Introduce character and/or problem*)	**Middle** (*Show problem or show character* trying *to solve the problem*)	**End** (*Show solution*)
Zoe is lonely and wants a dog.	She asks her parents who say no.	She asks for a fish instead, and they say yes.

Beginning (*Introduce character and/or problem*)	**Middle** (*Show problem*)	**Middle** (*Show problem happening again or show a character* trying *to solve the problem*)	**End** (*Show solution*)
Zoe is lonely and wants a dog.	She asks her mom who says no.	She asks her other mom who also says no.	She asks for a fish instead, and they say yes.

Assessing Students' Understanding of Planning a Story

Though I generally collect students' folders once a week, there are certain times in a unit when I collect everyone's work regardless of where we are in the week. Planning is one of those places. Before I teach students to move from their plans to their drafts, I want to see what those plans entail so I can address urgent issues before students move too far off-track. It is one thing to ask a young writer to re-do her plan; it is quite another to ask her to re-do a draft she has potentially spent days creating. (If some of our students started drafting stories prior to teaching them how to plan, we may expect them to plan and draft a new piece once we get to this step of the unit, especially if their initial draft lacks the focus that often comes with a plan.)

When we collect students' draft plans, we not only want to assess whether students have a plan; more importantly, we want to assess whether those plans depict realistic, focused, and meaningful stories. We might include the following lenses on our assessment chart: no draft plan; story not realistic; beginning does not connect with the story; ending does not connect; and/or confusing sequence of events.

In addition to collecting their plans, we will informally assess students' understandings during lessons and conferences. We will also watch them after the mini-lesson to notice whether students return to their seats and immediately start drafting, or whether they first take the time to plan. The following list of questions and corresponding supports can help guide our assessment and follow-up teaching:

Do students plan their stories before drafting?

:: When we see students jump into drafting without planning, we might simply remind them of our mini-lesson and tell them to try it themselves.

:: Or, if we think one of the other strategies in this section would be better suited to a particular writer, we might teach a new way to plan.

Do students' plans reflect a fictional yet realistic story about a believable character, problem, and solution?

If not, see ideas in the assessment sections on pages 45–46, 50, and 54.

Do students' plans include a beginning or an ending that does not connect with the rest of the story?

If so, see the ideas under the assessment question on the bottom of page 78.

Are students' plans focused with a clear beginning, middle, and end? Can you clearly envision the stories that will unfold from those plans?

:: Teach students to tell their stories across their fingers.

:: Teach students to tell each part of their stories in a single sentence.

:: Teach students to use sequence words: first, then, next, and finally.

:: If students' stories go on and on without clear direction, give them a limit of three central events, one each for the beginning, middle, and end, and help them try again. Remind them to show their problem in one of those events and their solution in another.

:: If a written plan lacks focus or clarity, ask the student to tell you how the story will go. Some young writers simply need help breaking a cohesive vision into three respective parts.

:: If certain parts include nothing more than a feeling ("She was happy"), teach students to plan for an action, as well. Characters should *do* something in the beginning, middle, and end of a story.

Are students' plans *too* detailed?

:: If the goal is for students to plan what the major event will be in each part of their stories, but they are instead planning every detail, teach them to think about the most important thing that happens in the beginning, middle, and end.

:: Teach students to write or say one short sentence for each part (the beginning, middle, and end) of their stories. (Some students will have two middle scenes in which case they should describe each one with a sentence.)

Are students' plans underdeveloped—not detailed enough?

:: If the goal is for students to tell a strong story before they write it, but their oral stories do not include the types of details we want them to include on the page, teach them to tell their stories again with new information. For example, you might have them include feeling words in the beginning, middle and end; or you might have them include in each part something a character says or thinks.

:: If students include just feelings with no actions in certain parts of their stories, teach them that something has to happen in the beginning, middle, and end.

How Two Students, Ellen and Alexa, Created Characters and Planned for Their Drafts

During the first week of her class's realistic fiction unit, Ellen creates a character. Typical of kindergartners, she only puts a few traits in writing and spends time developing her character through her picture details. Also typical, she sometimes confuses inside and outside traits, as we see when she put "glad" outside her character and "happy" inside and outside her character. However, especially at Ellen's age, it is less important that she records traits in the appropriate place and more important that she generates a variety of character details. From Ellen's character chart, we know the following: Her character is a ten-year-old girl named Elena. She has short, dark hair. She wears dresses. She plays with her friends. She is happy and glad. Were I to confer with Ellen at this stage, I would teach her to also consider her character's wants and fears both so we know more about her character on the inside, and because those details can help her generate possible problems. (See Figure 4.8.)

Elena

Outside traits	Inside traits
She is 10	*Happy*
Happy	
Glad	
Plays with friends	
Short, dark hair (depicted in drawing)	
Wears dress (depicted in drawing)	

Figure 4.8—Ellen's character chart, kindergarten

Once Ellen created a character, she considered problems and solutions. Ideally, she would have generated at least two or three possible problems and corresponding solutions. Instead, Ellen lists one problem and solution, shown in Figure 4.9, before planning her story.

Problem	Solution
Her friends don't want to play with her	She asks her friends and they say yes we will play with you

Figure 4.9—Ellen's list of problems and solutions, kindergarten

Finally, Ellen plans her story, shown in Figure 4.10. Because it is time-consuming for most kindergartners to compose even a small amount of text, and because Ellen's class already used a graphic organizer to brainstorm problems and solutions, she and her classmates planned their stories by telling each part across pages and then sketching those parts. Ellen does produce a focused draft (shown in the next chapter); however, the drawings in her plan are similar enough to one another to make me wonder how effectively they could remind her of her plan. When students produce plans like Ellen's, I teach them to add setting, people, and/or object details to help them distinguish each part.

p. 1 "This is Elena."   p. 2 "Her friends don't want to play with her."   p. 3 "She asks them and they say yes."

Figure 4.10—Ellen's sketched plan for her realistic fiction story, kindergarten

By first grade, most students can produce more writing, as shown by Alexa's generating work. First, Alexa creates two characters (versus one) with a variety of inside and outside traits, though like Ellen, she sometimes confuses inside and outside traits. Alexa's character charts show a shift away from drawing and toward writing details. (See Figure 4.11.)

Laney

Outside traits	Inside traits
A girl	Likes science experiments
Yellow hair	She has a best friend
Brown eyes	She wants a cat
Long eye lashes	Likes to go outside

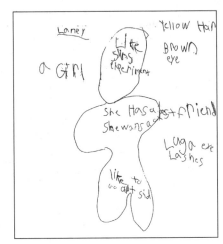

Figure 4.11a—Alexa's character chart, first grade

Suney

Outside traits	Inside traits
I am a girl	*She fixes things*
Her mom owns a restaurant	*Likes lots of animals*
9 years old	*Had a guinea pig*
Blue eyes	*From China*
Brown skin	*Wants a dog*
Brown curly hair	

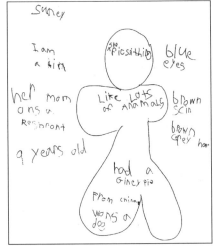

Figure 4.11b—Alexa's character chart, first grade

    After spending a few days creating characters, Alexa spent time considering problems and solutions. She used two different graphic organizers to first brainstorm possible problems and then possible solutions. Ideally, Alexa would have generated solutions for more than one problem, though she successfully lists more than one problem and solution. (See Figure 4.12.)

Character	Problem
Suney	Wants a dog but her mom and dad won't let her have one
Suney	Suney was riding her bike. Her friends were making fun of her. She doesn't know how to ride a two-wheeler.

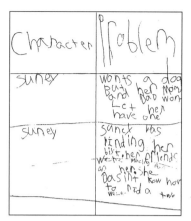

Figure 4.12a—Alexa's list of problems, first grade

Book	Problem	Solution	Solution
Suney rides a bike.	Her friends were making fun of her.	Her sister could help.	She could try by herself.

Because Alexa's class spent two days using graphic organizers to generate problems and solutions, they did not use another graphic organizer to plan their stories. Instead, as in Ellen's class, they planned their stories by telling and then sketching each part across pages. Alexa's plan clearly depicts what she plans to write in each of her three parts: in the beginning, she plans to introduce her character, Suney; in the middle, she plans to show Suney trying to ride a bike; then she plans to show her friends making fun of her; at the end, she plans to show Suney learning to ride a two-wheeler. (See Figure 4.13.)

Figure 4.12b—Alexa's Problem and Possible Solutions chart, first grade

p.1 "Introduce character, Suney"   p.2 "Suney rides a three-wheeler."   p.3 "Her friends make fun of her."   p.4 "Suney learns to ride a two-wheeler."

Figure 4.13—Alexa's sketched plan for her realistic fiction story, first grade

CHAPTER 5

Drafting

Overview

During drafting, which will likely last three to five days, I have three primary goals. I want students to:

1. Consider thoughtful ways to begin and/or end a story.
2. Write with detail.
3. Write with focus.

After all of their hard work—all their thinking and planning and imagining—our students are finally ready to write their stories! Your classrooms will likely brim with excitement on the first day of drafting, bringing a new wave of energy. Before we embark on the next stage of the unit, we'll want to organize our materials. By now, we should have a mentor text, but if we don't, we'll want one on which we can rely, especially during differentiated instruction (Anderson, 2000). We'll also want a complete draft of our own realistic fiction story, again, something we can use as a model during whole-class and differentiated instruction. (You can use the sections in this chapter on using our own writing to help you compose your story.) Finally, we need to stock our writing center with new paper choices to support students as they move from generating ideas and planning to drafting.

When it comes time to draft, I encourage teachers to create booklets by stapling together three to four pieces of paper (depending on the number of parts most students included in their plans; students can of course add additional pages as needed). Booklets encourage students to write each part of their stories on a different piece of paper, which supports several goals. If students have a blank page for just the beginning, one for just the middle and so on, it encourages them to elaborate each part. Using separate pages also helps students stay focused; they are more likely to pause at the end of each part if they need to turn to a new piece of paper, which means they are also more likely to attend to what comes next in their plan, rather than letting their writing get away from them and carry the plot in all kinds of unfocused directions. Finally, drafting each part on a separate page makes it easier to add, rearrange, and/or rewrite isolated parts when it comes time to revise.

Because I always offer students a variety of paper choices, I put at least two types of booklets in the writing center during drafting; I simply choose two or more types of paper already in the classroom, one with more lines than the other so booklets can support students at different levels. I also stock the writing center with individual sheets of paper so students can independently add more pages to their stories when desired. Remember that we can avoid "traffic jams" at the writing center by putting blank booklets on students' tables on the first day of drafting when we know everyone in the class will need one. From then on, students can independently go to the writing center when they need more paper.

Our options for which lessons to teach during drafting, as well as for how to sequence those lessons, are endless. In this chapter, I suggest four mini-lessons (to span four days) as *one* possible approach to drafting, knowing the series of mini-lessons will not feel appropriate for every reader depending on your group of students. (The italicized text beneath each lesson heading is a teaching point.) In Chapter 7, I offer additional strategies for drafting (as well as revising), so you can easily add to, exchange, and rearrange the lessons in this chapter to better support the students before you.

Day 1: Beginning the Draft

Writers often begin drafts with a lead that pulls readers into the story and makes them want to keep reading. One way to write an engaging lead is to use action and/ or dialogue to show what is happening in the beginning of the story. (For more ideas and strategies for crafting leads, see Chapter 7.)

As with everything we teach, we need to consider our students and their stage of writing development before we choose and plan the mini-lessons that will serve them best. In some classrooms, I would teach a simpler strategy for leads, such as beginning with the problem (see page 98). (Remember that if a teaching point doesn't feel appropriate for a whole-class lesson, you might have individual writers who would benefit from the teaching in a conference or small group.) But if students are ready to think about how to *craft* their lead in addition to what content to include, we might teach them to use dialogue and/or action. If students do not yet have experience using dialogue, we should teach it in isolation. Otherwise, we can teach both strategies (dialogue and action) in the same lesson. We might teach students to move between what characters say and do in a single lead. Or, we might teach them to imagine an action lead as well as a dialogue lead, and then to choose the one they like best. Either way, we can talk with students about how using dialogue and action helps pull readers directly into the moment, because it lets us hear and see characters as if we are in the room with them.

If we're teaching dialogue in isolation, we might say to students, "Rather than *telling* your readers what your characters are saying, you can write the exact words coming out of their mouths. So instead of writing, 'Zoe told her mom she was lonely,' we could write, 'Mama, I'm so lonely!' Zoe said.'" Though it may seem like an obvious shift to us, it often takes a lot of modeling and coaching on our parts, and a lot of practice by students before they begin to internalize this skill.

If students are already trying dialogue when they write, we can share a more sophisticated example of using dialogue. I might say, "I could start my story by writing, 'Zoe walked all over her house looking for someone to play with. She was lonely.' But instead, I want to try using dialogue to *show* what Zoe is doing and feeling in the beginning of my story. Maybe I could write, 'Hello?' Zoe called into the kitchen. But no one was there to answer her. 'Hello?' she called into her mom's study. But no one was there, either. 'Oh well,' Zoe thought to herself. 'Another day with no one to play with.' Do you see how the things Zoe says and does *shows* readers what she's doing (walking around the house looking for someone) and how she feels (lonely, maybe even a little bored)?"

Another way to build on students' knowledge if they are already using dialogue is to begin our lesson by saying, "Today we're going to talk about leads. Since so many of you are trying dialogue, I want to teach you that you can move between dialogue *and* action to show even more of what is happening. This is an excellent way to begin your stories because it allows readers to be in the room with your characters . . . ."

Moving between dialogue and action is an effective way to craft a lead, but it is also an effective way to show instead of tell what is happening throughout a story. In turn, if students are developmentally ready, we will likely teach and re-teach them to move between dialogue and action, revisiting the strategy multiple times in the unit for a variety of purposes, from crafting leads to writing with detail to crafting endings.

Using Published Texts to Teach Students How to Craft Leads With Dialogue and/or Action

When we teach leads (as well as endings), we often have to look to texts other than our mentor. When teaching something like details or focus, we can usually find multiple examples of the skill in a single text. But of course every story only contains one lead (and one ending). If our mentor does not begin the way we are teaching students to begin, or if we want to show more than one example of our strategy, we need to turn elsewhere.

The following examples include the published lead in addition to what the authors *could* have written were they telling instead of showing the beginning of their stories. I transcribe several sentences of each lead to show authors moving back and forth between what characters say and do. We could also simply show students the first sentence or two of a lead to exemplify just dialogue or just action.

Bunny Cakes, Rosemary Wells

Wells could have started her story by writing: *Max wanted to give Grandma an earthworm birthday cake, but Ruby wanted to give her an angel surprise cake.* Instead, Wells crafts a more engaging lead:

> *It was Grandma's birthday. Max made her an earthworm birthday cake.*
> *"No, Max," said Max's sister, Ruby. "We are going to make Grandma an angel surprise cake with raspberry-fluff icing."*

Peter's Chair, Ezra Jack Keats

Keats could have begun his story with the following: *Peter's mom told him to play more quietly because his new sister was sleeping.* Instead, he uses dialogue and action to show this event unfolding:

> *Peter stretched as high as he could. There! His tall building was finished. CRASH! Down it came. "Shhh!" called his mother. "You'll have to play more quietly. Remember, we have a new baby in the house."*

Whistling, Elizabeth Partridge

Partridge could have started her story with: *Jake's dad said it was almost time, and Jake came out of his sleeping bag.* Instead, she writes:

> *"Jake," Daddy whispers. "It's almost time." I poke my head out of my warm sleeping bag.*

Preparing Our Own Writing to Teach Students How to Craft Leads With Dialogue and/or Action

Try this: Create four columns on a blank page. Use your draft plan to think about what happens in the beginning of your story. In the first column, write one to three sentences (depending on the level of your students) that simply tell or summarize what happens. This can be your example of what *not* to do. Now consider what a character might do to *show* what happens in the beginning of your story. Write one to three action sentences in your second column. Next, consider what a character might say at the beginning of your story, and write one to three dialogue sentences in the third column. Finally, in the fourth column, craft a third way to begin your story by combining some of your action and dialogue sentences into a single lead. To show students moving back and forth between the two strategies, you might need to create a new action or dialogue sentence and intersperse it with ones you already have.

For example, I wrote four possible leads for my story about Zoe wanting a dog, the first being an example of telling, which is *not* what I want students to do in this mini-lesson. I can shorten each depending on the level of students for whom I am modeling:

1. Zoe didn't have anyone to play with, so she was lonely.

2. Zoe called her best friend on the phone but there was no answer. She asked her mom to play, but her mom had work to do. She looked around her empty house for something to do.

3. "I'm so lonely!" Zoe told her mom at breakfast. "I wish I had someone or something to play with."

4. Zoe called her best friend on the phone but there was no answer. "Mom, can you play with me?" she asked, but her mom had work to do. She looked around her empty house for something to do. "I'm so lonely!" Zoe told her mom. "I wish I had someone or something to play with."

Day 2: Writing Focused Stories

It is important to write focused stories so your readers always understand what is happening and how it connects with the rest of the story. One way to write with focus is to move back and forth between our plan and our draft, since we already made sure our plans were focused. (For more ideas and strategies for writing with focus, see Chapter 7.)

When students start writing their stories, you may want to encourage them to stay close to their plans—especially if we notice them losing themselves in the writing and forgetting their plans altogether. Obviously, our goal is not to discourage creativity, but at this stage in their writing, it makes sense to keep them on track with their planning. There will be time during revision for them to veer off into spontaneous directions. You may feel the need to show students, step by step, how we *use* our plans to direct us as we draft. Rather than picking up paper and writing, writing, writing until they get to the end of their stories, we want our students to slow down. We can show them how, at the beginning of each part of our story (the beginning, middle, and end), we stop, reference our plans, and think. We might ask some of the following questions to help us get our minds ready to write with focus: What is my plan for this part of my story? What happens in this one part? What happens at the beginning and at the end of just this part (because I want to be sure I don't start or end off-track)?

Paper is important in this lesson. We have already given students stapled booklets and shown them how to write each part of their stories on a separate page. We now want to show them how, when we stop and think before writing each part of our story, we also make sure we know where we will write that part. If we are about to start the middle, we need to make sure we turn the page of our booklet and begin on a fresh page. If we run out of room, we can always add more paper to our booklets, rather than combining parts (for example, the middle and the end) on a single page.

As with anything we teach, demonstrating pitfalls can help students internalize what we want them to do (and not do) and why. "I finished my beginning," I might say. "I still have some room on this paper, so I'm going to keep writing from here. Let's see, I left off with Zoe thinking about how she wants a dog. So I'll just keep writing: *Her best friend has a dog, so she calls her up, too—*" But then I stop writing and look up. "Uh-oh, wait a minute. I just remembered I'm supposed to write each part of my story on a new piece of paper. This is supposed to be my middle, not my beginning, so I better cross this out and turn the page to a fresh sheet. And you know what else? I never even thought about my draft plan! I know how my story goes, but I also know I'm supposed to really *use* my draft plan before I write each part or I could get off track. I better look at what I planned . . . Wow, my sketch shows that in the middle, Zoe asks her parents for a dog and they say no. There isn't anything about her calling her friend! I'm glad I used my plan or I would have had to rewrite the middle of my story! Let me try again . . . ."

Using Published Texts to Teach Students to Move Back and Forth Between Their Plans and Their Drafts

Because this teaching focuses on a writing *process* rather than a tangible product, we are better off using our own writing and thinking (as I do above) to teach students how to use their draft plans. Though we could show students an example of a focused story that honors its draft plan, that would be far less valuable than showing them how we navigate the process of getting to that end product.

Preparing Our Own Writing to Teach Students to Move Back and Forth Between Their Plans and Their Drafts

Try this: Get a blank booklet to start a new draft of your story, as well as an additional piece of blank paper, which I will refer to as the "research page." As you write your story in your booklet, move between your plan and your draft, but more importantly, try to notice (research) as much as you can about what you are doing as a writer. For example, pay special attention to any time you stop to think about what or how to do something, or any point at which you feel stuck. These, especially, are the moments we want to highlight for students, so use your research page to record your thinking at these times: Why do you stop to think? What goes through your mind? How do you get unstuck? Also record the things you do that you expect to be tricky for students, either because they may skip the step altogether or because they won't know how to proceed.

For example, will your students remember to pause periodically and check their plans? Will they know what to do if they start to write their middle on the first page of their booklets, but then catch their mistake? What about when they start drafting on one day and then return to their drafts a day or more later? If you teach your students to use their plans as a strategy for writing with focus, you can use the notes you take on your own process to help you model the key moves and pitfalls that you want to highlight.

When I sit down to draft my story, the first thing I do is look at my plan to make sure I know where my story starts. Because I think a lot of students won't do this, I record this move on my research page: *Looked at plan to remember where to start writing.* When I return to my draft, I write about how Zoe is lonely and wants a dog. I start writing about her asking her mothers if she can have one, but then I stop because I don't remember whether I'm supposed to do that on my first page or in the middle of my story. I look at my draft plan to remind myself. Again, I expect many students won't do this, so I write: *Paused to reference plans because wasn't sure where to end part one.* When I look at my plan, I find that I've written too much; I'm not supposed to show Zoe talking with her parents until the middle of my story. I spend some time thinking about what to do now: Should I change my draft plan? No! I know it's focused and meaningful, so I don't want to change it in the middle of drafting. Should I cross off what I've written and rewrite it on the next page? If it were only a few words, I would do that, but I've written more than I want to rewrite. Instead, I get a pair of scissors to cut my first page in half and tape the part about Zoe asking her parents for a dog onto the second page of my booklet. On my research page, I write: *Wrote two different parts on one page. Could rewrite things on the right page. But I cut and pasted because it was more than I wanted to rewrite.* I keep drafting and researching myself, recording potentially tricky parts until I reach the last part of my story.

Day 3: Including Details

Writers include details in their stories to help readers experience what characters experience. One of the most important ways to write with detail is to let readers know how characters feel during each part of the story. (For more ideas and strategies for adding important details, see Chapter 7.)

One of the very first ways I teach writers to include details is by letting readers know how characters feel. Even our most emergent writers can convey character emotion through their pictures. Once students are putting words on the page, they can tell readers how characters feel by simply stating the emotion. Gigi, a first grader whose individual learning plan affords her additional literacy support, does a beautiful job conveying emotion; she tells readers how her character feels and, because she does so at each turn of her story, Gigi also lets us know when those feelings change. See Figure 5.1 for her story.

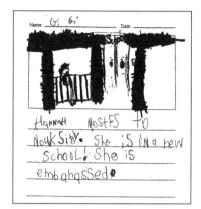

Figure 5.1—Gigi tells how her characters feel, first grade

Once writers are telling readers how their characters feel, we can teach one or more of a variety of strategies for showing how characters feel: through facial expressions, body movements, actions, dialogue, inner thinking. Notice, in Figure 5.2, how Phin begins to use dialogue, in addition to speech bubbles, to show how his characters feel. For example, on page 4 he writes: "What should I do?" he said to himself. "Who should I ask? What should I do?" Reading this, I know the character feels confused. On page 5, when Phin writes, "Yes!" in a speech bubble, I know his character feels excited and happy.

Hannah moves to a new city. She is in a new school! She is embarrassed.

Hannah goes in the new school. She is feeling a little better. She goes in the office. She is going in to the new class. She is going in fifth grade. She is 11.

She knocked on the door.

She waited there. She felt nervous. She took a few deep breaths.

The bell rang. She went to the new class. The teacher said, "Welcome to our new class." The kids were nice to her. One of the kids said hi to her. She felt happy.

It was time for lunch. She ate a sandwich. She ate with her friend. It was time for recess. Her friend played with her. She felt good!!

Figure 5.2—Phin shows how his characters feel, first grade

Max wants a skateboard

Once there was a boy that really, really wanted a skateboard for Christmas. He can't wait for Christmas. It was 4 days away. He didn't know if Santa would bring a skateboard. And he didn't know what to do. And he lived on 38 Finn Street. He lived with his 2 dads. (Speech bubble: I want to have a skateboard.)

It was Christmas. "I really want a skateboard." After they opened the presents he didn't get it. "Rrrr! I am mad!" (Speech bubble: Rrrr!)

"What should I do?" he said to himself. "Who should I ask? What should I do? Let's see. Oh, I know, I could do chores so I could get the money so I could buy one." (Speech bubble: Yes)

"Dad," he said, "what chores can I do?"

"Mmmm, I know," and his dad handed him a list. After he did all the chores he had a lot of money. He went to the store. He went to the toy aisle and he bought the skateboard. (Speech bubble: Yes!!)

After he bought the skateboard he couldn't wait to open it. When he got home he rode it. It was such fun.

The internal story (including how characters feel) is what brings meaning and significance to external events. So whatever the strategy, as soon as writers understand how to structure the events of a story, I want them to include how characters feel about those events. In most of our students' realistic fiction stories, those feelings will change as characters move through problems toward solutions. We can therefore also teach students to ask themselves with each turning of the page, "What are my characters feeling *now*?"

Using Published Texts to Teach Students How to Convey Character Emotion

Before we teach students to include their characters' emotions, we need to clarify for ourselves the specific strategy or strategies we want them to practice. I include an example of several different strategies from each of the texts below:

When Sophie Gets Angry—Really, Really Angry . . ., Molly Bang

:: Bang lets readers know how her characters feel by telling us: *Oh, is Sophie ever angry now!*

:: Bang shows her characters' feelings through the pictures: On the first page, both characters are smiling, so we know they are content. On the second page, Sophie's expression changes, letting us know she is upset.

:: Bang shows feelings through dialogue: We know Sophie is upset when she shouts, "*No!*"

:: Bang shows feelings through characters' actions: We know Sophie is angry when Bang writes: *She kicks. She screams.*

My Friend and I, Lisa Jahn-Clough

:: Jahn-Clough occasionally tells us how characters feel: On page 13, she writes: *We were very happy.*

:: Jahn-Clough shows emotion through her pictures: On page 12, the characters are smiling so we know they are happy. On page 17, they look angry. On page 18, they look shocked.

:: Jahn-Clough shows emotion through dialogue: On page 19, we know the boy is angry when he says, "*You're not my friend anymore . . . Go away.*" On page 26, we know the girl feels badly when she says, "*I'm sorry I broke your bunny.*"

:: Jahn-Clough shows emotion through her characters' actions: On page 16, we know the friends are angry when Jahn-Clough writes: *I pulled the bunny. My friend pulled it back. We grabbed and shouted and yelled and pulled.*

Goal!, Mina Javaherbin

:: Javaherbin tells us how characters feel throughout her story. For example, she writes: *When we play, we forget to worry. When we run, we are not afraid . . . When we play, we feel strong.*

:: Javaherbin shows emotion through word choice. For example, she writes: *We are real champions, playing with a real ball.* And later: *We run after our brilliant ball.* The words "real" and "champions" and "brilliant" convey a sense of pride and excitement. When the bullies come, she writes: *We are trapped.* The word "trapped" conveys fear.

:: She shows emotion through the character's actions. When the bullies arrive, we know the narrator is nervous and scared when Javaherbin writes: *I do not breathe and nod yes.* We know Jamal feels similarly when Javaherbin writes: *Jamal covers his face with his hands.*

:: Javaherbin also shows emotion through a combination of dialogue and action. We know Badu is frustrated when Javaherbin writes: *Badu jumps and shouts, "No way. No goal when the bucket falls."*

Preparing Our Own Writing to Teach Students How to Convey Character Emotion

Try this: Think about how your character feels at the beginning of your story. Write it down and draw a picture of your character that shows the appropriate emotion. Now act out what you do with your face and your body when you feel this way. Write a couple of sentences that show your character doing those same things. Finally, imagine your character is talking to another character or thinking something in her head; what could she say or think that would show readers how she is feeling? Depending on the level of your students, write a speech bubble or a sentence or two of dialogue. Now organize some of your free-writes into one or several sentences (depending on the level of your students) that let readers know how your character feels. Repeat these steps later in your story when your character's emotional state changes.

For example, in the beginning of my story, Zoe feels lonely. I could write that and draw a picture of a girl with a slight frown and droopy eyes. When I act lonely, my shoulders slump. I rest my chin in my hands and pout my lips slightly. I sigh. Zoe is alone in the beginning in my story, so she can't talk to another character. But if she were thinking something, she might simply think, "I'm lonely!" Or, she might long for company, thinking something like, "I wish I had someone to play with." I could synthesize some of these ideas into the following passage: *Zoe was lonely. She slumped her shoulders, rested her chin in her hands, and sighed. "I wish I had someone or something to play with!" she thought to herself.*

Day 4: Addressing Your Convention Goal(s)

Teach a lesson that addresses your convention goal(s) of the unit. I address conventions briefly in Chapter 3 and encourage readers to teach one convention about every four to six mini-lessons. Especially if you have not taught one for several days, you might do so during drafting. For example, depending on your students, you might teach one of the following:

:: *Writers use periods when we write to let readers know when to stop, take a breath, and think about what they just read. One way to know where to put a period is to say a complete thought in our head and write it down with a period at the end; then repeat with the next complete thought you have for your story.*

:: *Writers use the word wall when we write to make sure we spell everyday words correctly.*

:: *When we're not sure how to spell something, we can say the word slowly, listening to each sound we hear at the beginning, middle, and end, and writing the corresponding letter.*

:: *Writers often use a variety of end punctuation when we write. In addition to using periods to let our readers know when to stop and think, we use question marks at the end of a question so our readers know to read a sentence as a question. We also use exclamation points when we want our readers to read something with excitement or energy or more volume.*

:: *Writers punctuate our dialogue by putting talking marks (quotes) before the first word and after the last word a character says or thinks. This lets our readers know to read those words in the voice of the character.*

Assessing Students' Understanding During Drafting

As always, we will informally assess students during lessons and conferences, but we will also collect and assess their finished drafts, so we can plan for the next steps of the unit: revising and editing. If students have multiple drafts (which they may not), we need to teach them to pick one of those pieces to bring to publication. I usually model for students how I look through every piece in my folder, each time asking myself a few questions: Do I really care about this piece? Do I want to share it with others? Do I feel like I can do more work to make it even better than it already is? Students should pick one piece about which they can say, "Yes!" to all queries. Of course, when students only have one story, we don't need to teach this process.

When we collect students' drafts, we can again use a chart to help guide our assessment and determine our follow-up instruction. As always, what we put on the chart will depend on what we have taught, though we might also include concepts we are considering teaching but are unsure students need—for example, if we haven't addressed endings but are considering doing so during revision, we will first want to see whether students need help with endings. Our assessment chart may include some or all of the following: beginning, middle, and end of the story connect; relevant details; told feelings; shown feelings; dialogue [or speech bubbles]; stretched problem or solution; thoughtful lead; thoughtful ending; setting; and whatever convention(s) is the focus of our unit. Once we've assessed the stories students will bring to publication, we can use our chart to plan for our whole-class mini-lessons and differentiated instruction. The questions and supports below can help guide our assessment and follow-up teaching:

Do stories go on and on, making you wonder what is happening or why it is happening? Do you wonder about the relevance of certain parts?

:: Help students take apart their booklets and lay each part on the floor in order. If parts are combined on the same page, cut the pages so students have a separate pile for the beginning, middle, and end of their stories. Now teach students to move in order through their piles, using their draft plans to help them first tell each part of their stories, then revise and/or finish their written versions to make sure they match their focused, oral narrations and draft plans.

:: Ask students to summarize their beginning, middle, and end across three fingers. Make sure their summary is sequenced and focused. Ask students to re-read the beginning of their stories, pointing to everything that goes with the first finger of their retell and underlining everything that does not. Repeat for the middle and end of their stories. If students find that some of the underlined parts can be moved elsewhere, help them do so; if not, have them cross out those parts.

:: If students are trying to squeeze each part of their stories onto one page, or letting one part spill into the next to fit everything onto three pages, help them add more paper to their booklets.

Do students begin or end with something that does not directly connect with their story?

(For example, does the character wake up or go to sleep, even if that event is not relevant to the problem or solution?)

:: Tell students to revisit their draft plans and say what happens in the beginning or end of their stories (whichever part lacks focus in their drafts). Teach them to put themselves inside that moment and ask: What is the very [first or last] thing that is happening here? Teach them to revise their lead or ending so it honors what is meant to happen.

:: Tell students to revisit their draft plans and say what happens in the beginning or end of their stories. Make a timeline for them, with the point in time they just shared (the lead or ending) as well as the problematic lead or ending in their draft. Show students how their [lead or ending] occurs either before or after it should.

:: Tell students to briefly summarize the beginning, middle, and end of their stories across three fingers, coaching them toward a sequenced and focused retell. Teach students to check their written leads or endings against the ones they told on their fingers.

Do students have multiple strategies for writing with detail?

:: If students do not have any strategies for writing with detail, teach them to write down how characters feel as they draft each part of their stories.

:: Guide students through telling their stories orally. Teach them to choose one part of their stories and tell it across three fingers. Then teach them to tell that same part again but with new detail; for example, you might model how you add feeling words or dialogue to your story, or how you stretch each action across two fingers instead of one, so that you are now telling the same part of your story across six fingers. Once students have retold the same part two or three times with more and more detail, tell them to write those parts with the same rich detail—and to practice similar work as they draft other parts of the story.

:: If students are squeezing their writing into limited paper space, teach them to use different paper and/or to use multiple sheets for each part of their stories so they can make each of those parts as long as possible with as much detail as possible.

:: Have students share their stories with each other to notice something one of their classmates does that they could try in their own pieces. Remind students that when we read as writers, we notice (and emulate) craft not content.

:: Teach students to revisit familiar published texts to notice one or more things an author does that students want to try in their own stories.

:: In conferences or small groups, name what students are doing well and teach them another way to write with detail. (For additional strategies you might teach to help students use important details, see Chapter 7.)

Do students include details that connect with the problem and solution and hence with the intended meaning of the piece?

:: Teach students to hold onto what they want their readers to know and feel during each part of their stories. As they compose or re-read each sentence, they can ask, "Does this have anything to do with my problem or my solution?" If not, teach students that it probably doesn't belong in this particular story, and they should delete it.

Do students write one part of their stories with a lot of detail, but fail to develop other parts of their stories? Or do students fail to develop important parts of their stories with enough detail?

:: Name for students one or two strategies they already use for writing with detail and show them examples in their stories. Then encourage them to use those same strategies to develop other parts of their stories.

:: Teach students to identify especially important parts of their stories, such as when the problem or solution occurs. Then teach them to make those parts more detailed than other parts in their stories, either using a new strategy for details or strategies they already know.

:: If students are limited by their paper choices, direct them toward new paper. For example, if a writer is squeezing text onto paper with too few lines, teach them to use paper with more lines, and/or to use multiple pages for each part of their stories.

Are students thoughtful about their leads, or do they tend to begin all their stories the same way?

:: Teach students at least two ways to begin a story and have them write at least two different leads for the same piece. They might do this on two different pieces of paper; when they choose the lead they like best, they could then staple that page to the top of their story.

:: Teach students to act out the very first thing their characters do. On their own, or with the help of a partner, students can orally describe what they did, then use that information to craft their lead.

:: Teach students to revisit familiar published stories and to talk about what they notice and like about how they begin. Teach students how to try something similar with their own piece.

Do students' endings seem too abrupt?

:: Teach students another strategy for endings (see Chapter 7 for ideas). Students might write more than one ending, on two different pieces of paper, so they can choose the one they like best and staple it to the end of their booklet.

:: Teach students to act out the very last thing their characters do. On their own, or with the help of a partner, students can orally describe what they did, then try ending their stories in the same place and with similar detail.

:: Teach students to revisit familiar published stories and to talk about what they notice and like about how they end. Then teach students how to try something similar with their own stories.

Do students use developmentally appropriate conventions? Do they grasp the convention goal of the unit?

Depending on the convention, you might teach one or more of the following (Angelillo, 2002; Bender, 2007).

:: If students struggle with periods, you might teach them to:

- Read their stories aloud, listening for and adding a period in places where they take a breath.
- Check whether it would make sense to replace "ands" or "thens" with a period.

:: If students struggle with spelling, you might teach from the following, depending on their specific need and level:

- Use an alphabet chart to label pictures with initial sounds.
- Say each word aloud listening for beginning and ending sounds, and record the corresponding letters.
- Slowly say words aloud, stretching them like a rubber band to hear beginning, middle, and end sounds.
- Use the word wall.
- Use writing around the room or in a book if they can quickly and easily reference it.
- Try spelling a word two different ways in the margin or on another piece of paper and choose the one that looks best.

:: If you want to teach students to punctuate dialogue, you might teach them to:

- Put talking marks at the beginning and at the end of just those words coming out of a character's mouth.
- Open to a page in a published text, notice what expert authors do, and try one or two ways to punctuate dialogue (from quotes to commas to periods to paragraphs).

:: If students use periods fairly consistently and correctly and are therefore ready to use a variety of end punctuation, you might teach them to:

- Re-read their stories looking for at least one place where they want their readers to read with excitement or extra volume and add an exclamation point. Re-read stories again and see whether they are missing any questions marks—or perhaps whether they might add a question.

- Revisit a familiar published story and notice the different ways the author ends her sentences. Teach students to use those observations to try ending a few of their sentences in new ways.

How Ellen and Alexa Drafted Their Stories

Let's take a look at how Ellen and Alexa drafted their stories. See Figure 5.3 for Ellen's draft, which she took two days to write. Ellen's piece shows evidence of all the learning she has done in the unit thus far. She incorporates character details from her chart into her lead. She has a clear beginning, middle, and end, as well as a clear problem and solution. On her second day of drafting, she staples a fourth piece of paper to her booklet and stretches out her ending with new details, including how her characters feel about the events ("They had fun."). Ellen uses dialogue to show readers what is happening. She sometimes uses periods when she writes, and she even starts using quotation marks to punctuate her dialogue. Future learning for Ellen includes telling readers how her characters

Figure 5.3—Ellen's realistic fiction draft, kindergarten

This is Elena.
She is 10.
She likes to play with her friends but her friends do not want to play.
She asks her friends and they say, "Yes we will play with you."
They go to Elena's house to play. They had fun.

This is Sunny. She still rides a 3 Wheeler. She really wants to be able to ride a bike.

Sunny was riding her bike. Her friends were . . .

making fun of her.

She went to Child's Park and she tried and tried and tried. She fell and fell and fell but at the end of the day she said . . . I can do it! And she did it.

Figure 5.4—Alexa's realistic fiction story, first grade

feel and including more information about how problems are solved. (In the next chapter, we see Ellen insert a blank piece of paper between pages two and three to add an event that makes Elena's friends change their minds about playing with her.)

Alexa took two to three days to draft her story, which is shown in Figure 5.4 and also reflects her growing knowledge as a writer. Alexa writes a focused piece with a clear beginning, middle, and end, each part of which connects with a clear problem and solution. She writes her middle across two pages and uses ellipses to build suspense. She also stretches out the problem on her last page by using repetition (". . . she tried and tried and tried. She fell and fell and fell . . .") and by writing a list of character actions. Alexa composes with a variety of punctuation (periods, ellipses, and exclamation points), and often uses punctuation to create voice and to convey character emotion.

Future learning for Alexa includes showing instead of telling what's happening. For example, she could use dialogue or inner thinking to show how characters feel; she could show an important event (like trying to ride a bike) by writing two or three sentences describing the smaller actions inside the bigger action; she could also use dialogue and action to show important events unfolding.

CHAPTER 6

Revising

Overview

During revision, which will likely last two to four days, I have one primary goal. Before students get ready to edit and publish their stories, I want them to revisit their drafts with attention to craft and find at least one or two places where they can improve the quality of their stories.

When I was a first-year teacher, my classroom turned chaotic in the days before publishing. Thinking I had to help students perfect their pieces before we made them public, I literally spent entire days helping student after student revise and edit their work. The problems with my approach were many-fold: I helped students fix their pieces rather than teaching them how to be better writers. I aimed for perfect examples of writing rather than improvement across the year. I met with individual writers, usually more than once, rather than with small groups. I have since learned the importance of seeing each unit as another stepping stone toward student growth rather than a test for perfection. And, I have learned the effectiveness and efficiency of targeting small groups of learners versus individuals.

Once we've assessed the stories students will bring to publication, we can use our chart to plan for our whole-class mini-lessons and differentiated instruction. Because we only have two to four days before students publish, we need to prioritize our teaching. Many of our students will need additional support in several areas. For those of us deeply committed to our students and to the work we do as teachers, we can easily feel disenchanted in the last days of a unit. When we have taught strategies for leads and details and focus, and yet our students have not yet internalized these skills, we can feel that our teaching has fallen short; we might even be tempted to extend the unit in the hope of attaining those more "perfect" pieces. Instead of focusing on what our students are not doing, I encourage teachers to look for growth. Perhaps students' leads fall short, but do we see evidence that they are trying new ways to begin than before? Maybe their stories are not as detailed as we would like, but are they more so than the personal narratives they wrote prior to this unit?

Our challenge now is to remember that this is one unit (we will have other opportunities to teach many of these skills and strategies) and to prioritize our teaching, so we can move to new units of study. We should choose two or three teaching points that feel most pressing for the majority of students for our whole-class mini-lessons, and we should choose one or two teaching points that feel the most pressing for each individual for our conferences and small groups. In order to maximize the number of students with whom we can work during this crunch time, we'll want more than ever to do small-group strategy lessons versus individual conferences whenever possible.

Our teaching during revision encompasses logistics as well as content; we need to consider whether students know how to organize their revisions, or whether we need to teach them how to physically add and/or rearrange text. In some classrooms, we can tuck logistics into a lesson on content, or perhaps address it during middle-of-the-workshop teaching. In other classrooms, we may need to devote an entire mini-lesson to logistics. We might implicitly (by modeling it inside a content lesson) or explicitly teach some

Jackson is 3 and he likes to dress up as a vampire all the time. His sister was mean. Really, really mean. His sister was pulling his hair. He felt hurt. (Speech bubble: AAAAH)

He was begging for a brother. So they adopted a little boy. "Hip, hip hooray!" he said.

Figure 6.1—During revision, Rowan added what is now the second page of his story, kindergarten

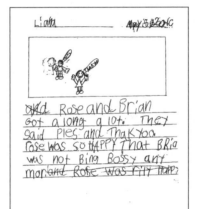
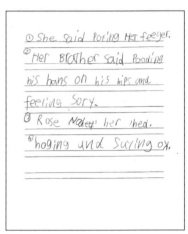

Figure 6.2—Liana kept track of additions by inserting a number in the body of her text and, on a blank page, new content next to the corresponding number, first grade

Brian Being Bossy

(Speech bubbles: Character #1—Brian said I want cookies. Character #2—I think he is being bossy.)
Rose lives with her mom, dad, and her brother. Her family lives on Mountain Street. One day Brian wanted to eat cookies. Her brother told Rose, "I want cookies!" She was silent.

He yells, "Rose, I want water!" Rose thinks he is being bossy. He is being bossy to Rose a lot. He is so bossy Rose took three deep breaths. That helped her.

She tells her mom and dad and she talks to her brother. She said, "You know you are bossy to me do you know that?" <u>she said, pointing her finger.</u>

"No, I do not know that," <u>her brother said putting his hands on his hips and feeling sorry.</u>

"Well you are being bossy." <u>Rose nodded her head</u>.

"No I didn't know, sorry."

"That's okay but do not do it ever again okay?" <u>[Rose said] hugging and saying okay</u>.

Rose and Brian got along a lot. They said please and thank you. Rose was so happy that Brian was not being bossy any more.

of the following: using carets to add a word or two; using sticky notes when we want to add more words than fit in the margins or between lines; inserting new, blank pages in the beginning, middle, or end of a booklet when we want to add a new part; keeping track of additions by inserting a number in the body of the text and, on a blank page, new content next to the corresponding number. See Figures 6.1 and 6.2 for examples of logistical moves during revision; in the transcript of each figure, I underline the text students added during revision.

When we teach revision, we need to use our own or student writing so we can show students what it looks like to make changes to a draft. We can still use published texts as the first step to our teaching—we might show a published example of the strategy we are teaching, then show students how to use that strategy to revise a draft. When using our own writing, we might write a less-than-perfect draft on chart paper and ask students to watch as we revise our piece; we could then ask them to help us revise the next part. When using student writing, we can show students the before and after version of their work, highlighting the changes and consequent impact.

Though the logistics change as we move from drafting to revising, the content is essentially the same. Often, we teach a set of strategies during drafting, and then during revision, re-teach strategies for which our students need additional support. Or, we might use revision to teach key strategies we did not have time to address during drafting.

As with drafting, the options for which lessons to teach during revising, as well for how to sequence those lessons, is fairly endless. In most classrooms, we will spend two to four days revising realistic fiction pieces. In this chapter, I offer one possible approach to revising that spans two days, knowing the lesson sequence will not feel appropriate for all classrooms. (The italicized text beneath each lesson heading is a teaching point.) In the following chapter, I offer additional strategies for revising, so you can easily add to, exchange, and rearrange the lessons in this chapter to better support the students before you.

Day 1: Adding Detail to Our Stories

Writers often revise our stories by adding more detail. One way to add detail is to stretch the problem—or attempts to solve the problem—across multiple events and multiple pages. (For more ideas and strategies for writing with detail, see Chapter 7.)

Whether students are writing each part of their stories in one sentence or twenty, teaching them to add a new part gives them a very concrete, accessible strategy for writing with more detail, as well as for revising text. Stretching the problem, or the characters' attempts to solve the problem, builds tension and consequently deepens readers' engagement.

When we teach this lesson, we first have students imagine the characters' efforts to solve the problem. For example, if someone falls down and their mother brings them a bandage, what else could the character do to try and solve the problem before it actually gets solved? Perhaps they could cry and call for help. Maybe they could then get up and look all around for help: in the kitchen, bedroom, or backyard. Each of these two events could be additional parts in a story. As students generate one or more new parts, they will add a new page to the appropriate place(s) in their booklets for each of those events.

Second grader Kiara receives additional support during reading and writing because of her special needs as a learner. During the realistic fiction unit, she integrated her learning and used it to produce a meaningful, focused, and detailed story. During revision, one of the strategies she tried was adding a new piece of paper to her draft in order to elaborate and better show her character's efforts to solve the problem. See Figure 6.3 for Kiara's story. In the transcription, I underline the added page.

Using Published Texts to Teach Students How to Stretch or Solve the Problem

When we use published texts to teach this strategy, we can emphasize for students how authors tend to stretch their problems and attempted solutions across several pages. We can again share what an author *could* have written and how much less engaging the story would be as a result.

Bunny Cakes, Rosemary Wells

Wells could have summarized the problem and Ruby's attempts to solve it on a single page by writing: *Max keeps spilling the ingredients for Ruby's cake, so Ruby keeps sending him to the store.* Instead, Wells stretches out the problem and solution across many pages: First, Max breaks the eggs, so Ruby sends him to the store for more. A few pages later, Max spills the milk, so Ruby sends him to the store again. In a few more pages, Max spills the flour, and once again, Ruby sends him to the store for more.

Owen, Kevin Henkes

Henkes could have summarized the problem and his characters' attempts to solve it by writing: *Owen's parents keep trying to get rid of Owen's yellow blanket, because it is old and dirty, but Owen always manages to keep it.* Instead, Henkes stretches the problem and solution across several pages: Toward the middle of the story, Owen's parents tell him to put the blanket under his pillow so the Blanket Fairy can exchange it for a wonderful new toy, but Owen hides the blanket instead. A few pages later, Owen's father

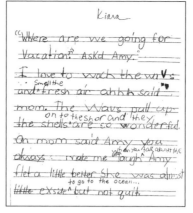

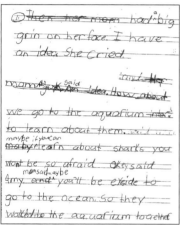

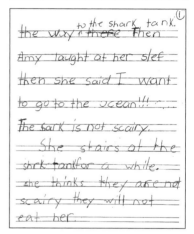

Figure 6.3—Kiara inserted what is now the fifth page of her story to stretch the solution, second grade

Amy's Problem *(Speech bubble: Help!!)*

"Where are we going for vacation?" asked Amy.

"I love to watch the waves and smell the fresh air, ahhh," said Mom. "The waves pull up the shells on the shore and they are so wonderful."

"Oh Mom," said Amy, "you <u>always</u> make me laugh when you talk about the beach." Amy felt a little better. She was almost excited to go to the ocean . . . but not quite.

"Do you want to go to the ocean?" said her mom.

Amy was shaking with fear. Then Amy said, "I am afraid of sharks. I do not want to go."

"So now, why are you so afraid of sharks?" asked Mom.

"Because they will eat me," said Amy.

Then her mom had a big grin on her face. "I have an idea," she cried. "How about we go to the aquarium to learn more about them. Maybe if you can learn about sharks you won't be so afraid."

"Okay," said Amy.

Mom said, "Maybe you'll be excited to go to the ocean." So they walked to the aquarium together.

Amy walked behind her mom quietly. She is still nervous. When she was walking she thought about puppies and she felt more safe. Finally they got there. Amy held her mom's hand on the way to the shark tank.

<u>She stares at the shark tank for awhile. She thinks they are not scary. They will not eat her</u>.

Then Amy laughed at herself then she said, "I want to go to the ocean!!!" The shark is not scary.

dips Owen's favorite corner of the blanket in vinegar, so Owen finds a new favorite corner. Finally, Owen's mother makes handkerchiefs out of the blanket, and now Owen always carries one of those with him.

My Best Friend, Mary Ann Rodman

Rodman could have summarized the problem and attempts at a solution by writing: *Lily keeps trying to get Tamika to notice her and be her friend, but Tamika ignores her.* Instead, Rodman stretches the problem and Lily's attempts to solve it across multiple pages and scenes: In the beginning, Lily says hi, trying to get Tamika's attention, but Tamika ignores her. A couple of pages later, Lily gets a new swimsuit like Tamika's to be more like her, but now Tamika has a new suit, too. Later in the story, Lily learns to dive to impress Tamika, but when Lily does her best dive ever, Tamika isn't even paying attention.

Preparing Our Own Writing to Teach Students How to Stretch or Solve the Problem

Try this: Find the problem on your draft plan or in your story. Can the problem repeat itself somehow in a new scene? If so, add a new box to your plan or a new page to your booklet and make a note of the new event. (If you think your students can plan for two additional scenes, do the same.) Now find the solution. Can one of your characters attempt to solve the problem before actually succeeding? If so, add one or two new boxes to your plan or pages to your booklet and make note of the event(s) you will add. (In some stories, it works to repeat the problem as well as characters' attempts to solve it. In others, one or the other makes more sense.) For example, one of my original plans reads as follows:

Zoe is lonely and wants a dog.	She asks her parents who say no.	She asks for a fish instead and they say yes.

I could stretch out the problem by adding one or both of the following:

Zoe is lonely and wants a dog.	She asks her parents who say no.	*They pass puppies in a pet store window, and she asks again. But they still say no.*	*She says she will save her allowance to pay for a dog and do all the work herself. But they still say no.*	She asks for a fish instead and they say yes.

I could also stretch out attempts to solve the problem by adding one or both of the following:

Zoe is lonely and wants a dog.	She asks her parents who say no.	*She uses her allowance to buy a stuffed dog.*	*She goes to a pet store to look for other ideas for a pet and notices the fish.*	She asks for a fish instead and they say yes.

Day 2: Revising Our Endings

Writers often revise our endings to make sure they are as meaningful and engaging as possible. One way to write a strong ending is to let readers know how characters feel now. (For more ideas and strategies for creating effective endings, see Chapter 7.)

Teaching students to end with an indication of the characters' emotions reinforces the importance of letting readers know how characters feel *throughout* a story. By asking students to reflect on an internal character shift, the strategy also implicitly teaches students that something always changes in a story and that often, changes occur inside characters. Finally, it teaches students a concrete, accessible way to end their stories with meaning, for ultimately, what characters experience internally is even more significant than the external events.

Depending on the level of our students, we might teach them to write a single ending sentence that tells readers how their characters feel now. Or, we might revisit familiar strategies, like using speech bubbles, dialogue, facial expressions, and so on, and teach students that they can end by *showing* how their characters feel.

Using Published Texts to Teach Students How to End With Characters' Feelings

Remember that when we teach students how to end stories, we often need to look to texts other than our mentor text for examples. Before choosing a text to teach this lesson, consider what, exactly, you want to teach your students to do: tell or show emotion. In some stories, such as *When Sophie Gets Angry—Really, Really Angry . . .*, authors end by *telling* readers how characters feel. In others, such as *Timothy Goes to School* and *Fireflies!*, authors *show* character emotion.

When Sophie Gets Angry—Really, Really Angry . . ., Molly Bang

And Sophie isn't angry anymore.

Timothy Goes to School, Rosemary Wells

On the way home Timothy and Violet laughed so much about Claude and Grace that they both got the hiccups.

Fireflies!, Julie Brinkloe

The moonlight and the fireflies swam in my tears, but I could feel myself smiling.

Preparing Our Own Writing to Teach Students How to End With Characters' Feelings

Try this: Consider how your character feels at the end of your story, after the problem is solved. Even if feelings from earlier in the story linger, has there been a shift of some kind? Depending on the level of your students, you might write a single ending sentence that simply states your character's emotional state.

If you teach more sophisticated writers, think about something your character could say, think, or do to show how he feels. Think of yourself when you feel the way your character feels. What do you do with your face, hands, or other body parts? What words or phrases do you think or say, regardless of the circumstances, when you feel this way? Now put yourself in your character's shoes. Is there something more specific he might say or do in this particular situation? Depending on whether you are teaching dialogue, speech bubbles, facial expressions, body movements, or a combination of strategies, use the appropriate technique(s) to write a sentence or more that shows readers how your character feels.

For example, at the end of my story, my Zoe is happy because her parents are letting her get a pet. I could end by simply writing: *Zoe was happy.* Or, I could show how Zoe feels by ending with: *Zoe clapped her hands together, smiled, then ran over and hugged her moms. "Thank you, thank you!" she said.*

Assessing Students' Understanding During Revision

Because we already assessed students' drafts to plan for revision and editing, we may not collect them again before the end of the unit. If we do collect students' drafts in the midst of revision, we might simply record "revising" on our assessment chart to identify students who are yet to make improvements of any kind to their pieces. If we don't collect their drafts again until the end of the unit, we can use the rubrics at the end of the next chapter for a more formal assessment. We can use the question and corresponding supports below to guide our assessment and follow-up instruction during revision.

Do students independently revise their stories, or are they suddenly off-task and stuck?

:: As you teach new strategies during drafting and revising, add them to one or two ongoing charts: "Ways to Write With Detail" or "Realistic Fiction Writers Often Do the Following" or "Ways to Revise." Refer to the chart(s) often during workshop. For example, as you transition students from the mini-lesson to their independent writing, you might say, "If you get stuck today, remember you can also look at our chart, 'Ways to Write With Detail,' for ideas." Or during the middle-of-the-workshop teaching, you might point to each item on the chart and say, "Raise your hand if you tried number one, adding character feeling. Raise your hand if you tried number two . . ."

:: Tell students to pick one new strategy from the chart that they want to try, or try more of, and then briefly re-teach the strategy.

:: Make sure students know how to organize their revisions. If they don't, teach them one or two easy-to-manage techniques for adding new text: using carets or sticky notes, adding new paper, or using a number system to keep track of additions listed on a new blank page. (See Figures 6.2–6.3 earlier in the chapter for examples of revision strategies.)

:: Ask students to help you add details to a draft you have written. Students can turn and talk with one another about ideas they have for you. As you call on partners to share, show students how you incorporate changes into your draft. Then ask them to re-read their own drafts to see whether they could do similar work with their pieces.

:: Teach students to think of one more event they could add to their stories, most likely another example of the problem or of the character trying to solve the problem. Staple a new piece of paper into the appropriate places in their booklets where students can add their new part.

:: Guide students through revision. Briefly show them how you revise your draft, using a strategy they already know; you can revise for anything, from focus to details to endings, as long as you are using a familiar strategy. Then give students a few minutes to revise their own stories using that same strategy. Repeat the process two or three times, knowing that not every student will be able to try every strategy, but hopefully they can all try at least one.

:: Guide students through revising their stories orally. First, teach them to tell their stories across three fingers. Then, remind them of a strategy they already know for making their stories better (perhaps adding feeling words or rewriting a lead as dialogue or ending with a character's facial expressions to show how they feel now), and teach them to retell their stories using the strategy. Once they've orally revised their stories, give students time to add their new details to their written drafts. Repeat the process two or three times.

:: Teach students that revision means to re-envision, or to see differently, which often means rewriting. If one part of their story is significantly weaker than other parts and would benefit from a rewrite, replace it with a blank page and have students draft a new, better version, encouraging them to use everything they've learned about writing stories well.

:: Provide opportunities for students to share with and give feedback to their peers with a focus on where and how they might revise their stories. We can teach students to consider important questions as they listen to a story and what they might say to prompt peer writers. We might chart one or more of the following questions and/or prompts, along with a visual icon for non-readers, to help guide listeners:

- Do you know how the characters feel? If not, say to the writer: Can you add feeling words to your story? (We might draw faces with different expressions on our chart.)

- Do you know anything else about the characters, such as the way they look or what kind of people they are? If not, can you describe your character a little more? (We might draw a person with detailed coloring and clothing.)

- Can you see where the characters are? If not, can you describe where your story takes place? (We might draw a tree and a house.)

- Does the problem end quickly, or is it stretched out over more than one event? If not, can you add another page and show the problem happening again, or show another way that your characters try to solve the problem? (We might draw two or three unhappy faces in a row.)

How Ellen and Alexa Revised Their Stories

Let's take a look at how Ellen and Alexa revised their stories. See Figure 6.4 for Ellen's story: She adds page three during revision to stretch out her character's attempts to solve the problem. She also adds feeling words in the beginning of her story, and she adds the last page to let readers know how her character's feelings change. In my transcript of her story, I underline the parts she added.

See Figure 6.5 for Alexa's story: On page three, she adds several sentences that show Sunny's friends making fun of her. When she adds, "She was silent," Alexa shows how Sunny feels in response to that teasing. Alexa also rewrites the end of her story,

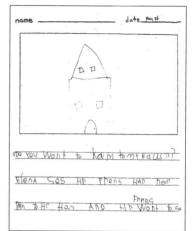

Figure 6.4—Ellen's revised realistic fiction story, kindergarten

This is Elena.
She is 10.
She likes to play with her friends but her friends do not want to play.
<u>She feels sad.</u>
    <u>"Do you want to come to my house?" Elena says. Her friends had never</u>
<u>been to her house and her friends want to go.</u>
She asks her friends and they say, "Yes we will play with you."
They go to Elena's house to play. They had fun.
<u>And she is happy.</u>

effectively moving between dialogue, action, and inner thinking to show her character solving the problem, as well as to show how her character feels as she first struggles and then succeeds. To highlight Alexa's revisions in my transcript of her story, I put a line through deletions and underline additions.

Figure 6.5—Alexa's revised realistic fiction story, first grade

This is Sunny. She still rides a 3 Wheeler. She really wants to be able to ride a bike.
Sunny was riding her bike. Her friends were . . .
making fun of her. <u>Ho Ho Ho! You still ride a 3 wheeler we ride 2 wheelers, Sunny! Sunny was silent.</u>
<u>Her friends were howling.</u>
She went to Child's Park ~~and she tried and tried and tried. She fell and fell and fell but at the end of the~~
~~day she said . . . I can do it! And she did it.~~
<u>She hopped on her bike and her bike ran and ran! She started pedaling! She fell. Ow!</u>
<u>Her knee got scraped. It was bad.</u>
<u>"1 more time," she said to herself. She got back on her bike.</u>
<u>And she did it. "Yay," she said.</u>

CHAPTER 7

Exploring Additional Ideas for Drafting and Revising

Because every school is different and every teacher unique, and because every school year brings with it a new mix of students with their own needs and passions, I do not believe in scripted curriculum. I believe in scripting a plan, yes. But I also think it essential that we revise our plans every time we put them into action with a new group of students.

Most likely, some of the drafting lessons in Chapter 5 and as well as some if not most of the revision lessons in Chapter 6 will feel too simple or too sophisticated for some of your students, or they will fail to fully address the particular goals you and your students have as writers. You can use this chapter as a reference guide for teaching leads, details, focus, and endings, turning to any of the four sections for additional strategies you might teach in lieu of or in addition to the strategies in Chapters 5 and 6. As always, some teaching points will feel more appropriate for whole-class mini-lessons, while others will help you address individual needs during differentiated instruction.

Creating Strong Leads

We all know the importance of a strong lead. Even our youngest writers likely know what it feels like to have a new story grip their attention from the first page, or make them lose interest before they get past the first few sentences. As students dig into writing, we want to teach them to consider their readers and how to lure them into the pages of their books.

When possible, I prefer to teach at least two ways to begin (and end) a piece. Doing so not only deepens students' knowledge base and helps remedy the predictable pattern of beginning every piece the same way; it also encourages students to consider what would work best for their particular stories. Depending on our students, we might teach two strategies in a single lesson, or one in our lesson and one during middle-of-the-workshop teaching.

If we teach leads as a drafting mini-lesson, we might say, "Let me first use my draft plan to make sure I start in the right place . . ." Briefly tucking this step into our teaching will support students with focus. If we teach leads as a revision lesson, we might teach students to staple a new piece of paper to the front of their booklets so they can write a new lead without trying to squeeze it into limited space. Students can either cross out their old lead on their now second page, leaving any other writing they may have done, or they can remove that page completely if they've rewritten the whole part.

Introducing the Problem

Teaching our youngest writers to introduce their problems in the beginning of their stories addresses two goals. First, it brings them back to the essential elements of a realistic fiction plot (the problem and solution), and hence helps them write focused, meaningful stories. Second, it teaches them an accessible way to lure their readers into their stories. When we encounter a problem in the first sentence of a story, we usually want to know more: What is going to happen *now*? What would I do in a situation like this? How will the characters respond to this challenge? We can teach our students that by instigating a train of questions in their readers' minds, they hold their readers' interests and keep them turning the pages of their stories for answers.

Of course, whenever we teach a strategy, we need to remember that it may not be appropriate for every student in the class, not simply because of level but because of what the student is writing. For example, if a student already planned to introduce their character in the beginning, show their problem in the middle, and show their solution at the end, expecting them to now introduce the problem in the beginning could undermine that plan. This is one reason why I prefer to teach multiple strategies when possible, even if it occurs across multiple days. It is also why I stress that each student needs to decide if and when to use something I teach in a whole-class lesson. (When I teach something in a conference or a strategy lesson, it is tailored to individual needs, and I am therefore comfortable telling students they need to try the particular strategy.)

Using Published Texts to Teach Students How to Introduce the Problem in the Lead

When considering how much of a story constitutes the lead, we can think back to the strategy we want to teach students and share just enough of the lead to clarify that strategy, as I do in the examples below. Doing so means that one sample lead may be a single sentence while another may be a paragraph or more.

How to Heal a Broken Wing, Bob Graham

High above the city, no one heard the soft thud of feathers against glass. No one saw the bird fall. No one looked down . . .

Bailey Goes Camping, Kevin Henkes

Bruce and Betty were bunny scouts. They were going camping. Bailey had to stay home.

William's Doll, Charlotte Zolotow

William wanted a doll. He wanted to hug it and cradle it in his arms and give it a bottle and take it to the park and push it in the swing and bring it back home and undress it and put it to bed . . .

Preparing Our Own Writing to Teach Students How to Introduce the Problem in the Lead

Try this: Consider the problem in your story. Write one to three sentences (depending on the level of your students) that explain that problem. *If* your draft plan says you will introduce the problem in the beginning of your story, this could be one possible lead. If you planned to do something else in the beginning of your story, you might create a new plan that fits with this lead. Or, you might use published or student writing to teach your students how to introduce the problem in their leads. You might use your own writing to encourage your students' independence, by showing them how you use your draft plan to choose a strategy for leads that works for *your* particular piece.

For example, the problem in my story is that Zoe wants a dog, but her parents say no. I could simply write that as my first sentence: *Zoe wants a dog but her parents say no.* If I wanted to model something more sophisticated, I could describe the problem with more detail: *Zoe really wants a dog. She wants something to play with and keep her company. But her parents don't want the extra mess or the extra work. Zoe is so disappointed.*

Adding Character Details to the Lead

Toward the beginning of the unit, students spend a couple of days creating and developing characters, but they often lose sight of those characters as attention shifts toward the plot. One way to help students develop characters inside their stories is through the lead. We can model for students the difference between including any details from our character charts versus details relevant to the plot. For example, in my story about Zoe who wants a dog, I might include in my lead the fact that she is an only child, her best friend lives far away, and her parents work a lot, because all these details affect Zoe's loneliness and hence her desire for a pet. Less significant are some of the other details on my chart: Zoe wears colorful clothes; she loves chocolate and baking; she talks fast. That said, especially when we teach kindergarten, we can applaud students' efforts to develop their characters when they open their stories with a list of extraneous details, much like we can applaud an emerging writer's efforts to use periods when she places one at the end of every line: both are examples of writers deepening their knowledge base, trying new things, taking risks, and making developmentally appropriate mistakes on the path toward more expertise.

Using Published Texts to Teach Students How to Add Character Details to the Lead

If the published text you've chosen as your mentor text does not begin with character development, but you would like to teach this strategy to students, remember that you can always reference a new text. You might choose from the examples below.

Sophie's Big Bed, Tina Burke

Sophie loves her crib.

Ruthie and the (Not So) Teeny Tiny Lie, Laura Rankin

Ruthie loved tiny things—the tinier the better. Her toys were the teeniest imaginable. She had dinky dinosaurs, itty-bitty trains, ponies no bigger than your pinky, and teddy bears that were barely there.

Melissa Parkington's Beautiful, Beautiful Hair, Pat Brisson

Melissa Parkington had the most beautiful hair anyone had ever seen. It was long, thick, black and so shiny it seemed to sparkle.

Preparing Our Own Writing to Teach Students How to Add Character Details to the Lead

Try this: Sort details from your character chart into two categories: ones that pertain to your story's problem and ones that do not. Make two columns on a blank page. Using the details that do pertain, craft one to three sentences about your character in the first column. In the second column, write a lead using details that do not pertain to your problem to show students the contrast of an ideal and less than ideal example.

For example, when I sort all the details on my character chart, I can use them to craft two different leads: *Zoe wears colorful clothes. She loves chocolate and baking. She talks fast.* Or, more relevant: *Zoe was lonely. Both her mothers worked a lot. She had no brothers or sisters. And her best friend lived far away.*

Adding Important Details

Once students finish their lead, the impulse is often to quickly summarize the rest of the story and be done—which leads to those plot-driven pieces we are trying to avoid. In kindergarten, the writers' level of development certainly yields more summary simply because students are writing less; a four- to six-sentence story will inevitably feel like a summary. But even in kindergarten, we can, and should, teach strategies for making those pieces more detailed. In most cases, this will mean adding a word here or a sentence

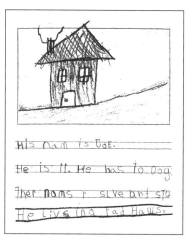

Homework trouble

His name is Joe. He is 11. He has two dogs. Their names are Steve and Stub. He lives in a red house.

Joe wants to go outside instead of doing his homework. Joe thought, "I don't want to sit inside. I want to go outside." Joe felt sad.

He does his homework and then he goes outside. Joe felt happy. (Speech bubble: Yay.)

Figure 7.1—Cazimir uses details to show isolated pieces of information, kindergarten

there, as Cazimir does in his story, shown in Figure 7.1. On the first page of his story, Cazimir lists several details about his character, just as we might expect a burgeoning kindergarten writer to do; the details do not directly connect with his story, and yet, they show evidence of his growing knowledge that realistic fiction writers develop their characters. As we turn the pages of his story, we see Cazimir including important character details that do directly connect with the story: On pages three and four, he tries inner thinking as a strategy for showing the problem in his story. On page four, Cazimir tells readers how his character feels in the face of his problem and then on page five, how those feelings change with the solution. Cazimir also includes speech bubbles on page five to show readers how his character feels. Cazimir does a beautiful job including details throughout his story, but he is still at the developmental stage of showing isolated pieces of information while summarizing the majority of his story.

Kate's draft, shown in Figure 7.2, is at another stage of development. Though some parts of her story still feel like a list, or a summary of events, she more consistently shows her characters doing and thinking and talking. For example, on page six, she writes: "She takes three deep breaths. She . . . steps into the train. She did it! 'I am proud of myself.'" When I read this part of Kate's story, I can see and feel and experience for myself what the character experiences; I see Kate standing at the entrance of the train and I feel her trepidation; I experience her courage, and then her pride and relief as she boards the train.

As students continue to grow and develop their skills as writers, teaching them to write with detail will extend beyond telling a detail here and showing a detail there. More and more, it will mean teaching students to craft each sentence differently, and to string those sentences together with new intention, so they can show their stories from beginning to end versus summarize events. In her story shown in Figure 7.3, Leah begins to move between dialogue, action, and inner thinking in a way that allows events to unfold on the page. When she revised her story, she revisited some (but not all) parts that were not quite effective scenes; she added action details to heavy dialogue between characters, so readers can see as well as hear what is happening in important moments. In the transcription of her story, I show Leah's revisions by underlining text that she added.

You might draw from the strategies below to help your students more along the continuum of first including more isolated details toward writing in scenes.

Include Speech Bubbles to Show What Characters Are Saying or Thinking

If students are not ready to incorporate dialogue into their stories, we can teach them to use speech bubbles as a step in that direction. Similar to when we teach dialogue, we can teach students to consider what characters might say aloud to another character as well as what they might say to themselves as an inside thought. We can also teach students different reasons for using speech bubbles, for example, to show the problem, the solution, and how characters feel.

Kate's Fear

This is Kate. She is scared of trains. But only if she could overcome her fear she would be happier.

One day, Kate's friends invite her on a train trip to New York City. But she is scared of trains. Kate thinks, "What should I do?"

She thinks about it for a week even in school. She talks to her moms about it. Kate thinks they're going on Monday.

Today is…? Monday. She thinks, "I have to go." She tells her mom, "I have to go." They run to the train station. They get there in time. She…?

She takes three deep breaths. She… steps into the train. She did it! "I am proud of myself."

She said, "I wanted to overcome my fears. I can face my fears!"

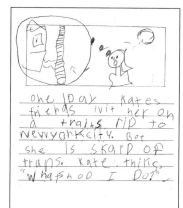

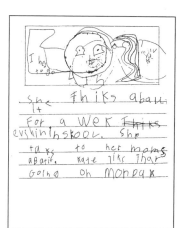

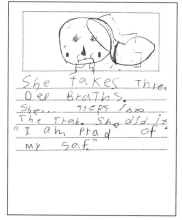

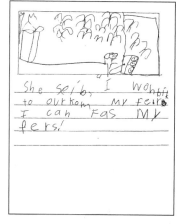

Figure 7.2—Kate begins to show instead of summarize events, first grade

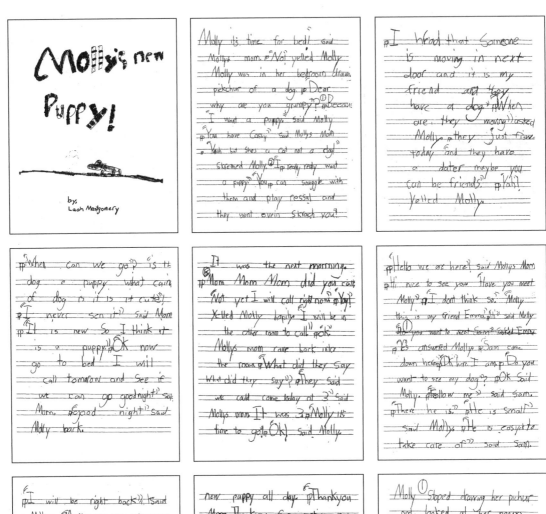

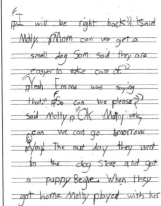  

Figure 7.3—Leah begins to write a whole story in scenes, second grade

Molly's New Puppy!

"Molly it's time for bed!" said Molly's mom.

"No!" yelled Molly. Molly was in her bedroom drawing a picture of a dog.

"Dear why are you grumpy?"

<u>Molly stopped drawing her picture and looked at her mom madly.</u> *"Because I want a puppy,"* said Molly.

"You have Cassy," said Molly's mom.

"Yeah but she's a cat not a dog!" screamed Molly. <u>Molly got off her bed and started stomping around her room.</u> *"I really, really want a puppy. You can snuggle with them and play wrestle and they won't even scratch you!"*

<u>Molly's mom stood up and looked happy.</u> *"I heard that someone is moving in next door and it is my friend and they have a dog."*

"When are they moving?" asked Molly.

"They just finished today and they have a daughter maybe you can be friends."

"Yah!" yelled Molly. <u>Molly started jumping around her room.</u> *"When can we go? Is the dog a puppy? What kind of dog is it? Is it cute?!"*

"I've never seen it," said Mom. *"It is new so I think it is a puppy. OK now go to bed. I will call tomorrow and see if we can go. Good night,"* said Mom.

"Good night," said Molly back.

It was the next morning. <u>Molly came running into the room.</u> *"Mom, Mom, Mom did you call?"*

"Not yet I will call right now."

"Yay!" yelled Molly happily.

"I will be in the other room to call."

"Ok."

Molly's mom came back into the room.

"What did they say, what did they say?"

"They said we could come at 3," said Molly's mom. It was 3. *"Molly it's time to go!"*

"Ok!" said Molly.

"Hello we are here!" said Molly's mom.

"Hi nice to meet you."

"Have you met Molly?"

"I don't think so."

"Molly this is my friend Emma."

"Hi," said Molly.

"Do you want to meet Sam?" asked Emma.

"Yes," answered Molly.

"Sam come down here."

"OK here I am. Do you want to see my dog?"

"Ok," said Molly.

"Follow me," said Sam. *"There he is."*

"He is small," said Molly.

"He is easier to take care of than a big dog," said Sam.

"I will be right back," said Molly.

"Mom can we get a small dog? Sam said they are easier to take care of."

"Yeah Emma was saying that."

"So can we please?" said Molly.

"Ok Molly we can go tomorrow." <u>Molly jumped all around.</u> *"Yay!"*

The next day they went to the dog store and got a puppy beagle. When they got home Molly played with her new puppy all day.

"Thank you Mom. Thank you for getting me this dog."

He is the best dog in the world.

Depending on which angle we take with our teaching, we might say, "Because most of you are doing an excellent job telling your readers how your characters feel, you're ready to learn something new. I want to teach you that writers often *show* how our characters feel, and one way to do this is with speech bubbles. This is a speech bubble," we can say as we show students an example from a familiar text. "Do you see how it's a bubble and it's coming out of the character's mouth? These words inside are what the character is either thinking in her head or saying out loud. When we want to show how one of our characters is feeling, we can make a speech bubble like this one, and then inside of it, write what our character would say or think when they feel a certain way. For example . . ."

If we want to teach another purpose for speech bubbles, we might instead say something like, "You all do a great job telling your readers what the problem and the solution are in your stories. Today I want to teach you that you can use something called speech bubbles to *show* something about the problem and/or solution. Let me show you what I mean . . ."

Using Published Texts to Teach Students How to Use Speech Bubbles

In some texts, such as *Knuffle Bunny*, authors use traditional speech bubbles with words inside an actual "bubble." In others, such as *Jessica*, speech bubbles look more like labels in that they are simply words on pictures without the bubble. What's important when looking for published examples is whether the text on the pictures reveals actual words characters are saying or thinking versus labels which might describe an object in the picture or an event in the story. If we want to highlight for students a certain purpose for using speech bubbles (such as showing feelings, problems, or solutions), we also need to identify the purpose in the examples we share with students, as I do in the examples below.

Knuffle Bunny Too, Mo Willems

Willems uses speech bubbles throughout his story. For example, on the way to school, Trixie is so eager to get there, Willems writes, *C'mon!* in her speech bubble to show how she feels. Later in the story, when Trixie and Sonja are arguing over how to pronounce the name of their identical, stuffed bunnies, Willems uses speech bubbles to show the problem; Trixie's speech bubble reads: *Kuh-nuffle! Kuh-nuffle!* And Sonja's speech bubble reads: *Nuffle! Nuffle!*

Jessica, Kevin Henkes

Throughout his story, Henkes writes characters' words and thoughts in his pictures. For example, on the opening pages, we see a picture of Ruthie with the words: *Jessica is my best friend.* When we turn the page, we see another picture of Ruthie with the words: *My toes are cold too, Jessica.* Both speech bubbles show the relationship between Ruthie and her imaginary friend, Jessica. They also show the problem, which is that people are concerned about Ruthie having an imaginary versus a real friend.

Horace and Morris Join the Chorus (but what about Dolores?), James Howe

Howe also uses speech bubbles throughout his story. For example, on the first page, Howe tells us that Horace, Morris, and Dolores love to sing; but he also shows this important character detail by giving each character a speech bubble that shows that singing: *LA LA LA LA LA LA LA LA*. In the middle of the story, after Dolores doesn't get into the chorus, her speech bubbles reflect her inner thinking, which shows the problem and how she feels: *I don't want to be in the audience!* And: *I want to be in the chorus.*

Preparing Our Own Writing to Teach Students How to Use Speech Bubbles

Try this: Use your draft plan to find where you introduce the problem. If your character is with another character, consider what they might say to each other to show the problem. If your character is alone, consider what he might think as he faces the problem. Sketch the character or characters and write those words or thoughts in speech bubbles. Now use your draft plan to find where the solution begins to unfold. Consider how your character feels and what he might say or think that conveys this emotion. On a new piece of paper, sketch your character again with a new speech bubble.

For example, I introduce my problem in the beginning of my story when I let readers know that Zoe is lonely and wants a dog. She is alone here, so I could sketch Zoe with a speech bubble of her inner thinking that reads: *I want a dog!* Or: *I wish I had a pet for company.* My solution unfolds when Zoe asks for a fish instead and her parents say yes. I could show how happy Zoe is by writing: *YAY!!* Or: *Oh, thank you, thank you!*

Move Back and Forth Between Dialogue and Action to Craft Scenes That Show What Is Happening

In the previous chapter, I introduced the movement between dialogue and action as a strategy for leads; and I explained that if our students are ready for this work, we will likely revisit it repeatedly across the unit—for example, as a strategy for writing with detail. When we do so, we can introduce to students the concept of scenes, which is one of the most effective ways to steer students away from producing plot-driven summaries.

Writing in scenes means showing (instead of telling) events unfolding on the page, so readers can enter into a story and feel like we are experiencing the moment alongside characters. Though scenes usually include a variety of details, moving between dialogue and action is a concrete and highly successful strategy for writers just beginning to grasp how to write scenes. Still, because writing in scenes is sophisticated work, we will likely only teach this concept in second grade and in some first grade classrooms; and even then, our goal is for students to *approximate* not perfect writing in scenes. See Figures 7.1–7.3 earlier in the chapter for a developmental progression toward writing in scenes.

We have already taken steps to support this foundational work: We have taught students to plan stories with a distinct beginning, middle, and end. We have also given them booklets versus individual sheets of paper to help them maintain that distinction, and to help them write each of those parts as long as possible. And in some classrooms, we have taught students that one way to begin a story is with dialogue and/or action.

If we teach second and possibly first grade, we might teach scenes as our first drafting lesson. We can show students how we refer to our plan, choose a part to draft, and then write it not as a single sentence or two that summarizes an event, but almost as its own, elaborated story. We might model with our own writing by saying things like, "Let me think: What was the very first thing my character said or did? Let me write that down. Now, what was the very *next* thing one of my characters said or did? I notice I have a lot of [dialogue or action] sentences. I'm sure my character was [doing or saying, either out loud or in her head] something, as well. Let me re-read and think about where I could show her [actions or words]."

Using Published Texts to Teach Students How to Craft Scenes

We often find multiple places in a single mentor text where the author uses dialogue and action to create a scene. We might pick two or three solid examples to share with students. We might also imagine for students how an author *could* have written a passage, were she or he summarizing. As always, the contrast of what we do and do not want students to do can help clarify our teaching. It can also help students grasp the effect of the strategy; in this case, we want them to experience how much more engaging a scene versus a summary can be for readers.

Sheila Rae's Peppermint Stick, Kevin Henkes

In the middle of his story, Henkes could have written: *Sheila Rae keeps teasing Louise. First she says Louise can have some of her peppermint stick if she can guess the number of stripes, but she tells Louise she guessed wrong; then she says Louise can have some if she can reach it, but Sheila Rae climbs up really high.* Instead, Henkes writes:

> *"You can have one lick, if you can guess how many stripes there are," said Sheila Rae.*
> *Louise thought and thought and thought. "Thirteen-seven," she said.*
> *"Wrong!" said Sheila Rae. "Too bad."*

"Please?" said Louise.

"You can have one lick, if you can reach it," said Sheila Rae. Sheila Rae climbed onto a stool and some pillows and some books.

Louise sighed. "Too high."

Ruby and the Copycat, Peggy Rathman

Toward the beginning of her story, Rathman could have written: *Angela and Ruby both told the class they were flower girls at their sisters' weddings. They started to become friends.* Instead, Rathman writes:

"I was the flower girl at my sister's wedding," said Angela.

"That's exciting," said Ms. Hart.

Ruby raised her hand halfway. "I was the flower girl at my sister's wedding, too."

"What a coincidence!" said Ms. Hart.

Angela turned and smiled at Ruby.

Ruby smiled at the top of Angela's head.

Ish, Peter H. Reynolds

In the middle of Reynold's story, he could have written: *Ramon yelled at his sister. She took his crumpled drawing and ran away, and he ran after her.* But instead he writes:

Ramon sneered. "I'm NOT drawing! Go away!" Marisol ran away, but not before picking up a crumpled sheet of paper.

"Hey! Come back here with that!" Ramon raced after Marisol, up the hall and into her room.

Preparing Our Own Writing to Teach Students How to Craft Scenes

Try this: Use your draft plan to think about what happens in the middle of your story (since we have already done some work with the beginning). Draw a vertical line down the middle of a blank page. In the left column, summarize the middle of your story in one or two sentences; you now have an example of "telling" from which we want to move students away. Now close your eyes and watch your middle as if it were a play. Hear the characters talking. See them moving. Pay close attention to their smaller movements: hand motions, facial expressions, body movements. What is the very first thing a character says or thinks or does in your middle scene? Write it down in the right column. Close your eyes again. What is the very next thing a character says or thinks or does? Write it down.

Whenever you write down a dialogue or inner thinking sentence, see the character *doing* something as she or he speaks or thinks. It might be a major action, or it might be something more subtle, like a facial expression or body movement attached to the dialogue. Whatever it is, write it down.

Whenever you write down an action sentence, consider whether you can break it down into two or three smaller steps, so your readers can see the action happening on the page; for example, instead of writing, "She fell down and scraped her knees," we might write: "She tripped and lost her balance. She reached out her hands to stop her fall, but landed hard on the concrete. Her knees scraped the pavement." Or, when you write an action sentence, consider whether you can add one more action sentence to describe the event with a little more detail. So if we wrote, "The friends yelled at each other on the playground," we might now add: "They screamed so loudly everyone turned to look."

Finally, consider and record anything the character might say or think in connection with their actions. You will likely shorten and simplify the text you create before you share it with students, keeping in mind that we want to write slightly above the level of the majority of our class.

For example, I can tell my middle scene as follows: *Zoe asked her parents for a dog and they said no.* I might compose the following as an example for students of showing:

> *"Mom, I think we should get a dog," Zoe said when she got home from school. Zoe put her hands together and begged, "Pleeeease?!"*
>
> *But without even giving it a thought, her mom said, "I don't think so, Zo. Dogs are a lot of work."*
>
> *Zoe crossed her arms and pouted.*

Include Character Details From Our Chart Inside Our Story

Though students spend a couple of days developing characters in the beginning of the unit, many of the details from their character charts never make it into their stories. Of course, many of those details have no place in their stories because they lack relevance to the plots that unfold. But, especially if we feel like the characters are underdeveloped in our students' stories, we might teach them to return to their charts and consider which details could be relevant.

If we have taught students to include character emotion, we might teach them to look to their charts for something their character might do when feeling a certain way. For example, if their character likes to dance, he might dance around the house when he is happy. We might also teach students to pick one or two details from their charts that they think they could tuck alongside something their characters say or do in their stories. For example, if their character has a pet, he might say a quick goodnight to it before getting into bed.

Using Published Texts to Teach Students How to Include Character Details From Their Character Charts

With this strategy, we are teaching students a process for thinking and making decisions as much as how to arrive at the end result. We'll therefore want to use our own or student writing, so we can highlight, as we move between a character chart and draft, how to make decisions about which additional details to include and how to weave them into a story.

Preparing Our Own Writing to Teach Students How to Include Character Details From Their Character Charts

Try this: Look between your character chart and a draft of your story so far (an incomplete draft should be fine). Consider how your character feels in the story. Could you add any details from your chart into your draft when your character is feeling a particular way in the story; for example, is there something she might do when she is sad and seeking comfort, or some way she might act when angry? Are there any other details on your chart that could fit in your story? As you read each detail, skim through your story in your mind and consider whether you might tuck new information alongside something your character says or does. Try to find at least two new details and add them to your draft.

For example, in the beginning of my story, Zoe is sad, so I look to my chart for something she might do for comfort. My chart says, "loves chocolate and baking; great artist; loves the ocean." I could write: *Zoe was so sad. She went to the kitchen to bake because it always made her feel better.* Or: *Zoe went to her room and took out her paints. She painted for a long time. She slowly started to feel a little less sad.*

My chart also says, "loves colorful clothes—pinks, oranges, and bright blues; quiet voice." Those feel like details that could find a place in my story, so I flip through my draft looking for an event to which I could attach them. When Zoe approaches her parents about a dog, I can write: *"Mom?" Zoe said in her usual whisper.* Later, when her parents say she can have a fish, I might write: *Zoe grabbed her favorite coat with pink buttons and bright blue pockets and ran out the door to the pet store!*

Include Setting Details to Let Readers Know Where Characters Are

If we teach setting, we might first expect students to show time and/or place in one part of their stories. Then, as with any other strategy for details, we can encourage them to weave information throughout. We might teach students to consider, with each turning of the page, "Where is my character *now*?" Whenever a change in time or place occurs, we can teach students to put themselves in their character's shoes and look around, considering one or more of the following questions: What does your character see? Does she see any objects or other people? What does she hear? Does she feel, taste, or smell anything?

In addition to teaching sensory detail, we might teach students that their characters can interact with their surroundings. We might ask students, "What could your character do that would let us know where he or she is, and maybe even let us picture some of the things around her?"

Depending on the learners before us, we can teach students to reveal the answers to setting questions through their pictures or their words. And regardless of the students before us, we want to make sure, as always, to name the specific strategy we are teaching—for example, using our senses or making characters interact with their surroundings.

Using Published Texts to Teach Students How to Develop Setting

We can use almost any picture book story to teach students to add setting details to their pictures. If we want to teach students to use their words to show the setting, we may have to look beyond our mentor text; many simpler stories that we rely on as mentors in the younger grades lack examples of setting developed through the words. If the mentor you've chosen is one such text, you might use one of the stories below.

Shortcut, Donald Crews

Crews shows the setting in a few places in his story. On the second page, he uses time clues and the sense of sight when he writes: *But it was late and it was getting dark.* A couple of pages later, Crews again uses the sense of sight to paint a picture of his characters' surroundings when he writes: *The track ran along a mound. Its steep slopes were covered with briers. There was water at the bottom, surely full of snakes.* Crews also lets us *hear* what's in those surroundings when he writes about the sounds the train makes: *Whoo-Whoo . . . WHOO-WHOO and KLAKITY-KLAK-KLAK-KLAK-KLAKITY . . .* Finally, the pictures let us know where characters are and when their setting changes: For most of the book, we see train tracks and trees and dirt road, but on the last page, we know the children are home because we see a house.

Ruthie and the (Not So) Teeny Tiny Lie, Laura Rankin

In addition to showing the setting through her pictures, Rankin helps us see where characters are by having them interact with their surroundings. For example, she writes: *One day at school recess, after jump rope and swings, Ruthie took a turn on the twirling bar. When she landed, she saw something in the grass.* Reading this, I see a more rural playground with grass versus concrete or wood chips, and I see a variety of play equipment and structures. Later, Rankin writes: *Ruthie . . . began the long walk to the front of the room. Mr. Olsen's desk seemed very far away.* Now when Ruthie interacts with her surroundings, I see a classroom with a walkway leading to the front of the room where a teacher's desk sits.

Whistling, Elizabeth Partridge

Partridge weaves extensive setting details throughout her story. For example, toward the beginning, she uses sensory detail (specifically touch and sight) to show where characters are: *The air is tingly and cold. Millions of tiny stars glitter in the sky.* She also reveals the setting by having characters interact with their surroundings. For example, when she writes, *I poke my head out of my warm sleeping bag . . . Daddy pushes another branch into the fire*, we see the characters camping in nature, surrounded by trees and sitting near a fire.

Preparing Our Own Writing to Teach Students How to Develop Setting

Try this: Where is your character in the beginning of your story? Put yourself in his or her shoes and use your senses to imagine several things about your character's surroundings: What do you see and hear? Do you feel anything, either because you touch it or because of the weather? Can you smell or taste anything? Now be a little more specific; instead of simply seeing a house, see a small, brown house with front steps and no yard. Finally, sift through the details and hold onto the ones that feel more relevant to your plot; if your story is about a boy who hurt himself at the playground, showing the small, brown house across the street is less important than showing the broken swing hanging by one chain. Draw a picture that includes at least two or three details that reveal the setting. Now write (or revise) the beginning of your story, making sure to include a sentence or two of sensory details that show the setting.

To try a third strategy, think about what is happening in the middle of your story. Where is your character now? (Perhaps in the same place.) Close your eyes and see your character interacting with one or two things in her environment. Write a sentence or two that shows this interaction and reveals the setting.

For example, in the beginning of my story, Zoe is in her house. If I put myself in her shoes and walk around the house, I see her room with an unmade bed, books and toys on the floor, and a small, open window. I feel a cool breeze because of the open window. I see a hallway with light blue, chipped paint and a beige carpet leading to her parents' room in one direction and to a kitchen and living room in the other direction; I know what each room is because of where I see beds, refrigerators, couches, and so on. I hear quiet: no voices, no one else's footsteps. I don't see any people or any pets. I can draw a picture of the inside of this house with the relevant objects and with Zoe, all alone. I might write: *Zoe walked through her empty house. She saw the books and toys in her room, but no friends or siblings to play with. She went into her parents' room, the kitchen, the living room, but neither of her mothers were anywhere to be found. Her house was so quiet, and Zoe was so lonely.*

In the middle of my story, Zoe asks her parents for a dog and they say no. I never considered where this scene unfolds, but once I focus on developing the setting, I decide to put my characters in the kitchen. When I close my eyes and picture Zoe interacting with objects in the kitchen, I see her sitting at the kitchen table, gripping her cup of milk because she is nervous. I see her foot tap-tap-tapping on the white linoleum floor. I might begin the middle of my story by writing: *Zoe sat at her kitchen table, nervously tapping the white floor with her foot. "Mom?" she asked . . .*

Writing With Focus

One of the most predictable problems that emerges when students try their hands at fiction is a lack of focus. Luckily, we took steps early in the unit to address this issue. We taught whole-class mini-lessons on generating and then choosing for each story topic a clear problem and corresponding solution. We taught the class to plan their stories, with a clear beginning, middle, and end, before drafting. We taught students to craft leads and endings that connect directly with the problem and/or solution in the story. We taught them to include details that similarly connect with the problem and solution.

Because students are sitting down to draft stories, day after day, with all this teaching in progress, we are less likely to find ourselves reading a stack of unfocused pieces. From the start, we have implicitly taught students to write with focus. But there may be times when the focus in students' stories begins to wane. The strategies below are for when we feel a need to *explicitly* teach focus.

Include Only Those Details That Connect With the Problem or Solution

Sometimes students are so focused on writing with detail that they lose sight of what their stories are really about. Perhaps their pieces are cluttered with unnecessary information, such as character details or events that do not connect with the plot. Perhaps they include details that undermine what they intend to convey, such as a character who smiles even though she has just fallen off her bike and hurt herself. Before we do anything, we want to congratulate students for trying new ways to write with detail. Not only does it mean they are taking risks, which we always want our young writers to do; it also means they are closer to understanding how to use details more effectively, for isn't it usually easier to do something well if we have practice, even if the practice is not yet perfect?

When we teach students to simultaneously attend to detail and focus, the first thing they need to consider is: What is my story about? And what is *this part* about? Then, as they compose or revise, we can teach them to hold on to the answers to those questions as they also consider new questions: Does this detail connect with what this is about? Does it help show my readers what I want them to know? Some students may need to move sentence by sentence through a story, making decisions about what to put on the page if they are drafting, or crossing off extraneous information if they are revising.

Using Published Texts to Teach Students How to Include Details That Connect With the Problem or Solution

Using our own writing will prove much more effective than turning to published texts, since finished products cannot show students the process of deciding which details to include and exclude. However, we could support the teaching we do with our own writing by re-reading some (during writing workshop) or all (during read aloud) of our mentor text to students, highlighting as we read how every single detail somehow connects back to the problem and solution.

Preparing Our Own Writing to Teach Students How to Include Details That Connect With the Problem or Solution

Try this: Think about a disconnected event you could add to your story. Insert a new page to the beginning, middle, or end and have your character do something like brush her teeth or go to the library for no relevant reason. Now choose another part of your story to rewrite with extraneous information. Copy the first sentence onto a blank page and consider a tangent you might follow. Write a new sentence or two that may relate to the first one, but does not relate to the central problem or solution. Keep reading the part of your story as it was originally written. Look for a person or an object or a place that you could describe with several details that may be rich but are nonetheless irrelevant, and weave them into your new, unfocused version of your story. When you teach this lesson, you can use what you just created by modeling for students how, as you re-read your draft, you hold onto what your story is about and cross out information that does not belong (namely, the information you just added above).

For example, I add a page with a disconnected event to the middle of my story, right after Zoe's parents tell her she can't have a dog: *Zoe was hungry, so she got out some cereal and milk. Her mom told her not to eat too much because it was almost dinner, so she only had a small bowl.* Then, I rewrite another part with extraneous details; I copy down the sentence that reads, *"Okay, how about a fish?" Zoe asked,* and I add: *Zoe's friend has a fish tank with three fish. She used to have four, but one died.* Finally, I look for a person, place, or object to describe; I choose Zoe's parents and brainstorm irrelevant details about them to weave into this part of my story, which now reads: *Zoe's moms thought for a minute. One of her moms has long, blond hair. Her other mom has short, curly hair and always wears dresses. She grew up in San Francisco, but now they all live in Massachusetts. Zoe's moms looked at her and said, "Sure! You can have a fish!"*

Crafting Good Endings

Leads are important because they lure readers into a story. Endings are equally important because they can make a story linger in our readers' minds long after they finish reading. As with leads, I always try to teach at least two strategies so students don't fall into the predictable pattern of ending all their stories the same way. I also want to make sure they understand that there is not only one right way to end a story. In fact, many endings employ a variety of strategies, especially if we look at the last chunk of text versus the last sentence or two.

In some cases, we might encourage students to try different endings for their stories and to choose the one they like best. Doing so, they may discover that only certain strategies work for their particular story. More importantly, they will gain another lesson in independence, learning that they always have choices as a writer, and that ultimately, that choice is theirs to make.

Use Action and/or Dialogue (or Speech Bubbles) to Show the Solution

Especially if we want to reinforce earlier teaching on writing with detail, we can teach students to conclude their stories with action and/or dialogue or speech bubbles. Some students may use our teaching to turn their solution into a scene, an event that truly unfolds on the page as characters move back and forth between speaking (or thinking) and acting. Others might use our teaching to craft a single sentence that concludes their stories with something a character says or does. Still others may not be ready to add dialogue to the body of their text, but could add a speech bubble to their final picture. Whatever the approach, the more students practice using dialogue and action, the more adept they will become at showing rather than telling important events to their readers.

Using Published Texts to Teach Students How to Use Action and/or Dialogue to End With the Solution

In each of the examples below, I transcribe enough of the ending to exemplify movement between dialogue and action. If you want to focus solely on action or solely on dialogue, you might share the very last sentence or two of a text—just enough to exemplify the strategy you are teaching.

Sophie's Big Bed, Tina Burke

> *"I think you might all like to sleep in this big bed," Sophie said. And so they did.*

Peter's Chair, Ezra Jack Keats

> *Peter sat in a grown-up chair. His father sat next to him. "Daddy," said Peter, "let's paint the little chair pink for Susie." And they did.*

King of the Playground, Phyllis Reynolds Naylor

> *"I'm going to build the biggest fort in the world," Kevin said, and began digging again.*
>
> *"Ha!" said Sammy. "It's got to have towers."*
>
> *"It will," Kevin said.*
>
> *"It's got to have a drawbridge," said Sammy.*
>
> *"It will," Kevin said.*
>
> *"It's got to have a ditch all around," said Sammy.*
>
> *"It will," Kevin said. "Help me build it?"*
>
> *"No," Sammy told him.*
>
> *But he did.*

Preparing Our Own Writing to Teach Students How to Use Action and/or Dialogue to End With the Solution

Try this: Close your eyes and watch the solution to your story unfold. You might play the whole scene to get fully in the moment, but then focus on how the scene ends. Are there multiple characters present? If so, what are they saying to one another? If there is only one character, what is she thinking? Making sure to skip lines, write down the dialogue (internal or external) that you hear. Especially if you teach kindergarten, you might instead sketch your characters and record some of their words or thoughts in speech bubbles. Close your eyes again to return to the end of your scene. Replay the conversation, but this time, pay close attention to what your characters are doing. Notice small actions as well as big ones: What do they do with their faces? Their bodies? Their hands? Write down some of what you see, using the skipped lines on your page to intersperse some of the dialogue with action phrases or sentences.

For example, the solution in my story is that Zoe asks for a fish instead of a dog and her parents say yes. When I close my eyes, I see Zoe standing in front of her two moms. Zoe says, "I was thinking that maybe I could have, well, maybe a fish instead of a dog?" Then her parents say, "Okay, you can have a fish!" And Zoe says, "Thank you, thank you! Can we go to the pet store *right now*?!"

When I replay the conversation, focusing now on what the characters are *doing*, I see

Zoe looking back and forth between her parents and squeezing her fingers because she is nervous. When she asks for a fish, I see Zoe's parents turn away from Zoe to look at one another. One mom lifts her eyes and her shoulders slightly, as if asking, "Why not?" The other mom pauses for a moment, then nods her head. Both smile at each other before they turn back to Zoe. Zoe has been squeezing her fingers this whole time and biting her lip. As soon as they turn back to her with a smile on their faces, she drops her hands and smiles, too. Zoe is already jumping up and down and clapping her hands when her parents say she can have a fish. Once she hears their answer, she runs up to them; she stands in between them and hugs their legs.

By weaving some of what I see my characters doing into what I hear them saying, I compose the following ending for my scene and for my story: *As soon as her parents turn back to her with smiles on their faces, Zoe smiles, too. "Okay, you can have a fish!" her parents say. Zoe runs up to them, and standing in between them, hugs their legs. "Thank you, thank you!" Zoe says. Everyone is smiling and hugging. "Can we go to the pet store right now?!" Zoe asks.*

Let Readers Know What Your Character Has Learned

In some stories, characters learn something very concrete, such as in Mo Willem's story, *Knuffle Bunny*, when Trixie learns to talk. And, of course, in many stories, characters learn lessons; perhaps they learn to share or to be kind or to try their best—or to take good care of the people they love, such as in Charlotte Zolotow's story, *Big Sister and Little Sister*. Though I do not suggest we teach students to turn every story into a moral, I do think every character learns something as they move through events, face obstacles, and overcome challenges. As students near the end of their stories, we might teach them to reflect on what their characters have learned, and to consider whether they want to conclude by imparting that knowledge to readers.

Using Published Texts to Teach Students How to End With What a Character Has Learned

When we teach this strategy, we need to briefly remind students what a story is really about by providing an *angled* retell: We do not need to revisit every detail in the story, but we should remind students about those events that lead to a character learning something at the end. For each published text below, I include a sample summary as well as a transcript of the ending.

Knuffle Bunny, Mo Willems

Summary: Trixie tries and tries to tell her father that she left Knuffle Bunny at the Laundromat, but because she hasn't yet learned to talk, her dad can't understand her. Eventually, they find Knuffle Bunny and Trixie is overjoyed. Willems ends his story by letting us know something important Trixie learns to do through all these events:

> *So Trixie's daddy*
> *decided to look harder.*
> *Until . . .*
> *"KNUFFLE BUNNY!!!"*
> *And those were the very first words Trixie ever said.*

Big Sister and Little Sister, Charlotte Zolotow

Summary: Big sister always takes care of little sister and does everything for her. When little sister runs away from home because she wants to do things on her own for a little while, big sister can't find her and cries. This time, little sister takes care of her. Zolotow ends her story by letting us know what little sister has learned from her big sister:

> *And from that day on*
> *little sister and big sister both took care of each other*
> *because little sister had learned from big sister*
> *and now they both knew how.*

One Green Apple, Eve Bunting

Summary: Farah is new to this country, and on the second day in her new school, her class goes on a field trip to an apple orchard. Farah notices and thinks about many things that are different in this country and her own, and she feels out of place. For one, she doesn't speak English yet, but she silently repeats English words in her head, too nervous to say them aloud. As the other children are kind to her, Farah slowly begins to feel a little more comfortable. Bunting ends her story by letting readers know what Farah is learning, namely, English, as well as comfort and confidence:

> *"App-ell," I say.*
> *Anna claps.*
> *I smile*
> *and smile*
> *and smile.*
> *It is my first outside-myself word.*
> *There will be more.*

Preparing Our Own Writing to Teach Students How to End With What a Character Has Learned

Try this: Consider what your character has learned. Has she learned to do something she couldn't do before? A new way to act toward or feel about others? Perhaps she has learned something about herself? Or about what is possible or impossible as she moves through the world? As you reflect on these questions, you will likely find that your character has learned many lessons. Choose one or two things your character has learned to which your students can relate. Write one to three sentences that end your story by letting readers know what your character has learned; you might even use the sentence starter, "[Character's name] learned that . . ."

For example, my character, Zoe, is lonely and wants a dog, but she gets a fish instead. Zoe could have learned any of the following: She can solve a problem if she keeps trying. Even when we don't get exactly what we want, we often get something wonderful. There are many, different ways to feel less lonely.

CHAPTER 8

Editing, Publishing, and Celebrating

When I was a classroom teacher, my students and I arrived at the final phase of a writing unit with a mixture of excitement and, to be honest, exhaustion. After weeks of thinking and planning and writing and revising, we were eager to celebrate our hard work. And yet, standing between us and the finish line was editing, rarely an exciting prospect for young writers. Especially because energy may be dwindling for you and your students, but also because we can only expect so much from our youngest writers when it comes to editing, I encourage K–2 teachers to move through the final phase of a unit quickly. And, more than ever, I encourage us to think hard about what is developmentally appropriate for our particular students as we develop a plan around our assessments and expectations.

Overview

During this stage of the unit, which will likely last three to four days, I have three primary goals. Before we conclude our realistic fiction unit, I want students to:

1. Edit (at least part of) their stories.
2. Make their stories more beautiful in preparation for sharing them with an audience.
3. Share their stories with an audience and celebrate their hard work!

Editing

Editing is comforting for many of us because it is so concrete. As teachers, we know a misspelled word when we see it. We can fix a run-on sentence or turn fragments into complete thoughts. Of course, our students don't know these things as well as we do, and we can't expect someone who doesn't yet know how to use periods to edit for periods. Editing is generally not the time to teach new conventions, nor a time to teach students how to use conventions as a way to play with craft (such as trying, for the first time, exclamation points to convey excitement). Remember, we have been weaving convention lessons throughout the unit, teaching a series of strategies to help students with periods or spelling or whatever our unit goal(s) may be. Different than teaching conventions, editing is generally a time to teach students techniques for finding and fixing things *they already know how to do*. Common editing lessons, which cut across genres and units of study, include:

:: Using an editing checklist to look for mistakes we know how to fix. (An editing checklist in kindergarten might include "spacing" and "word wall words," whereas one in second grade might include "spelling" and "periods and capitals.")

:: Making sure [whatever convention is your class' focus for this unit] is used correctly.

:: Using a peer editor.

:: Circling words we think are misspelled and using resources like the word wall and print around the room to fix the spelling we can.

:: Reading stories out loud, either to ourselves or a partner, to make sure everything looks right and makes sense.

Teachers often ask whether we should do a final edit for students before they move to publication. My concern is that fixing all the errors in a kindergarten, first grade, and often in a second grade piece can mean separating the writer from her work, not because someone else is making final corrections, but because those final corrections often leave the pieces of very young writers looking like nothing they could produce independently. We want students to see and celebrate *their* best work, and pieces with perfect spelling and conventions are very rarely an accurate reflection of what a kindergartner or first grader does independently.

Rather than our goal being "perfect" pieces, we might instead aim for pieces that reflect new growth. So when it comes to editing, we might target one convention need for each student. Even then, we probably won't have the time to work with every individual during editing. But by grouping students for strategy lessons, we can maximize the number of editing conferences we have. And then (are we ready for this?), let the other imperfections go for now!

Publishing

When it comes time to publish, the thinking and writing is essentially complete. Publishing is about making pieces as beautiful as possible (visually and orally) before they go out into the world. Students might illustrate and add a cover page to their stories. Most likely, they will color in their sketches. They might practice reading their stories aloud to themselves or a partner, working on fluency and volume, in preparation for reading to a larger audience during the celebration.

In classrooms (versus the real world of publishing), publishing generally happens quickly, in one or maybe two writing blocks. If your class spends one or two days on publishing, you might begin each day with a mini-lesson on one of the teaching points below. As with editing, the following cut across genres:

:: Writers often make our writing beautiful before sharing it with others by coloring in our drawings and by adding a cover page with our name, the title of our piece, and a drawing that connects with what our piece is about.

:: Before writers read our work aloud to an audience, we usually practice by first reading it aloud to a partner. With our partner's help, we can practice reading loudly enough and with fluency (meaning we read the punctuation and read at an appropriate pace, so our listeners can understand).

:: Before publishing, writers often add a dedication page at the beginning or a short biography of ourselves on an ending page.

Teachers often feel pressure to display perfect-looking pieces, even in the youngest grades. Another common question is whether we should type students' pieces, or whether students should rewrite their drafts after revising and editing them. I encourage teachers to consider developmental factors. First, how easy will it be for students to recopy their drafts? If it is going to take hours to recopy a story, it probably is not developmentally appropriate. Plus, all those hours spent copying means all that time lost for thinking and generating anew. And again, we may want to consider whether, after recopying stories without errors, students will still recognize them as their own creations. If not, they are less likely to see themselves as real writers, and less likely to trust that what they produce independently is, in fact, worthy.

Many teachers find it helpful to share expectations with families, along with an explanation of what is developmentally appropriate, so families better understand when and why their children's writing contains errors. If you send home a letter at the beginning of the year, you might also send home a reminder letter during publication so families are not startled when they see published pieces with errors. (See the appendix for a sample letter that you might send families in the beginning of the year.)

Once we take the above factors into account, we might expect some second graders to recopy their drafts, but likely not kindergarten nor first grade students; instead, their published pieces will look more like drafts, with all their revisions and edits and developmentally appropriate mistakes. On the other hand, we might, with select units during the year, type students' pieces for them. I suggest "select units," both because it again limits students' evidence of what they can produce independently, but also because it is incredibly time-consuming for teachers. That said, it can be exciting for students to occasionally have the experience of holding in their hands a polished piece of writing that they helped create. A balance of typed, polished pieces, alongside more authentic relics of their abilities, can help instill the sense of accomplishment and pride we strive for with all our students.

Celebrating

The Common Core State Standards states: "To build a foundation for college and career readiness, students need to learn to use writing as a way of . . . conveying thoughts, feelings, and real and imaginary experiences. They learn to appreciate that a key purpose of writing is to communicate clearly to an external, sometimes unfamiliar audience . . ." (Common Core Standards, 2010, 15) What an accomplishment that over the course of a few weeks, our students have moved from a simple sketch of someone with a make-believe name, to an actual, page-turning story with character thoughts, feelings, and experiences!

We want to conclude our realistic fiction unit by acknowledging all of our students' hard work. One way to do this is to provide an opportunity for them to make their work public in some way, just as writers in the world do upon publication. Doing so will also help students grasp the significance of writing for an audience. During the writing workshop that concludes our realistic fiction unit, we might invite outside friends and family, or another class, or a few building personnel selected by our students; or, we might enjoy a more intimate celebration with just our class. Whatever the audience, students might do one or more of the following:

:: *Be their character.* Students might interact with one another over celebratory snacks while talking or moving like their characters or wearing something (a color, an accessory, a particular piece of clothing) their characters might wear. Sitting in a culminating circle, students could share the character detail with their audience.

:: *Act out their stories.* Students might rehearse with their writing partners during publishing and then perform during celebration the problem and solution in each of their stories.

:: *Read their stories aloud.* Students might read their stories to buddies in another class, or to a small group of three to six people in their own classroom, whether it includes just their classmates or outside friends and family. If we want every attendee to hear from every writer, students might read a favorite page or two. (More than that, and the audience may get restless.)

:: *Display their work.* We might walk the halls with our students and their pieces in tow so that every writer can choose where she wants to hang her story. Beneath each piece, we might tape a piece of paper with the author's name, grade, and the genre. Or, we might hang everyone's pieces inside or just outside our classroom and briefly describe the work for passersby. We might also put our students' stories in a special "realistic fiction" bin in our classroom library so students can continue to read one another's stories long after the unit is complete.

Using Published Texts to Teach Students How to Edit and Publish

Though we might turn to published stories to show students how the authors use their best spelling and punctuation, we mostly need to rely on our own or student writing during editing, so we can show students how to fix errors, rather than simply showing them a final, polished product. During publishing, we can show students how authors include meaningful, beautiful pictures that match their words, including a cover page; we might also show them published examples of dedications and author biographies.

Preparing Our Own Writing to Teach Students How to Edit and Publish

Try this: Consider your students' knowledge of conventions. Where do they fall on the continuum of spelling development? What are developmentally appropriate goals for them when it comes to punctuation? What is your convention goal for the unit? Now take the realistic fiction story you wrote and rewrite the first few sentences with the types of errors your students often make but could edit on their own. For example, if my students spell phonetically, I might misspell "was" as "wuz" and use it as an opportunity to remind students to use the word wall; but I would not misspell "lonely" as "lonle" because the latter is phonetically accurate, and I wouldn't expect my students to use the conventional spelling for a word like "lonely." When teaching your students about conventions during whole-class or differentiated instruction, you can use the sample you create to model for students how writers edit for mistakes.

For example, let me imagine a class in which the following is true: Spelling is our convention goal for the unit. Most students record the beginning, middle, and end sounds in words. We have a word wall, though students often misspell these high-frequency words. They are beginning to explore periods.

I might write the following: *Zoe wuz lonely. Hr moms worked a lot she hd no bothers or siters hr best fend lived in da next town over so she only gt to see hr on weekends. Zoe decided da best thing to do wuz get a dog*

I could use the above to model for students how I slowly and carefully re-read my story out loud several times, first listening for places to add periods, then looking for misspelled word-wall words (such as "her" and "the"), and finally, looking for words where I left out a letter that corresponds with a sound I can clearly hear (such as "brothers" and "sisters").

Assessing Students' Understanding of Editing and Publishing

We might use a rubric at the end of the unit to assess students' published pieces so we can identify their accomplishments as well as the needs we might want to address in future units. The major difference between an end-of-the-unit rubric and the informal assessment charts we've used throughout is that the former might go home with students or be placed in their writing portfolios, whereas the latter is for our planning alone. Because formal rubrics become more public displays of students' efforts, they should only include things we have taught.

Because we want to assess what students can do independently, we need to consider whether to assess their published pieces or an earlier draft. If we type their stories without errors, or do a final edit for students and ask them to recopy their drafts, we'll get more insight into students' strengths and needs if we look at an earlier draft.

We might also teach students how to assess themselves as a way to help them develop ownership over their own learning. Self-assessments give us an opportunity to understand the accuracy of students' images of themselves as writers. Depending on their reading abilities, students might use a rubric independently, or we might ask students to rate themselves as we read one aloud to the class or to small groups.

Following are two sample rubrics you might adapt and use based on the particular work students did during your realistic fiction unit; one is for self-assessment and a second for teacher-assessment.

End-of-the-Unit Self-Assessment

What I accomplished	Yes	Almost	No
I wrote a focused story. The beginning, middle, and end connect.			
I let readers know how my characters feel.			
I stretched out the problem or attempts to solve the problem.			
I spelled word-wall words correctly.			
I used [another developmentally appropriate convention] correctly.			
I revised my story.			
I edited my story.			

End-of-the-Unit Teacher-Assessment

What the writer accomplished	Yes (1)	On the way (2)	No (3)
The writer made at least one character chart of someone he or she created. The character is fictional yet believable.			
The writer listed several possible problems and solutions that are fictional yet believable.			

What the writer accomplished	Yes (1)	On the way (2)	No (3)
The writer chose one character, problem, and solution and wrote a fictional yet believable story about them.			
The writer wrote a focused story. The beginning, middle, and end connect.			
The writer let readers know how characters feel.			
The writer used speech bubbles or dialogue.			
The writer stretched out the problem or attempts to solve the problem.			
The writer only included details that connect with the problem and solution.			
The writer began with a thoughtful lead.			
The writer ended with a thoughtful ending.			
The writer spelled word-wall words correctly.			
The writer used [other developmentally appropriate conventions] correctly.			

Teaching Young Writers to Craft Realistic Fiction

What the writer accomplished	Yes (1)	On the way (2)	No (3)
The writer revised the story.			
The writer edited the story.			
The writer made the story more beautiful during publication.			
The writer shared the story with an audience.			

How Ellen and Alexa Edited and Published Their Stories

Let's take a look at how Ellen and Alexa edited and published their stories. See Figure 8.1 for Ellen's published realistic fiction piece. During editing, she re-read her story for meaning, and on page three, she added the missing word, "friends." She also added a question mark on that page. Were I to confer with Ellen during editing, I might teach her to re-read for periods, listening for places she wants her readers to pause; or, I might teach her to look for and correct misspelled word-wall words, such as "her" and "want." That said, I think she accomplished plenty for a kindergartner! Though Ellen only made a few changes and mistakes remain in her piece, she independently re-read her draft and successfully found and fixed a couple of errors.

During publishing, Ellen colored in her pictures. Rather than rewriting her draft, Ellen devoted her time to her revisions and edits.

See Figure 8.2 for Alexa's published piece. During editing, Alexa added periods in several places. She also re-read for meaning and fixed her error on page five, where she initially wrote "when" instead of "were." Were I to confer with her during editing, I might teach her to re-read again looking for missing capitals at the beginning of sentences, though she only does this in a few places.

During publishing, Alexa made a cover page, wrote a dedication, and colored the pictures in the body of her story. Like Ellen, her published piece is, appropriately, her original draft with her revisions and edits.

Ellen's and Alexa's published stories show evidence of their understandings of realistic fiction, as well as their growing knowledge of the qualities of good writing. Over the course of the unit, both writers learned more about writing with focus and detail. They learned new strategies for leads and endings, they deepened their grasp of punctuation,

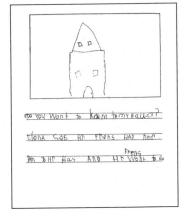

Figure 8.1—Ellen's edited and published realistic fiction story, kindergarten

This is Elena.
She is 10.
She likes to play with her friends but her friends do not want to play. She feels sad.
"Do you want to come to my house?" Elena says. Her friends had never been to her house and her friends want to go.
She asks her friends and they say, "Yes we will play with you."
They go to Elena's house to play. They had fun.
And she is happy.

and they developed their independence around revision and editing. Because they have learned transferable strategies for all of these skills, both authors can take their new knowledge with them as they venture into new stories, and even into new genres.

Equally significant is the fact that Ellen and Alexa, along with their peers, have

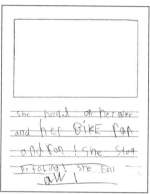

Figure 8.2—Alexa's edited and published realistic fiction story, first grade

Sunny Rides a Bike

This book is dedicated to my sister Olivia.

This is Sunny. She still rides a 3 wheeler. She really wants to be able to ride a bike.

Sunny was riding her bike. Her friends were . . .

making fun of her. Ho Ho Ho! You still ride a 3 wheeler we ride 2 wheelers Sunny! Sunny was silent. Her friends were howling.

She went to Child's Park.

She hopped on her bike and her bike ran and ran! She started pedaling! She fell. Ow!

Her knee got scraped. It was bad.

"1 more time," she said to herself. She got back on her bike. And she did it. "Yay," she said.

learned to honor and develop their imagination. When we teach students to craft fiction, we teach them to think beyond the realm of what is and to conceive of what might be—which means we nurture not only writers but visionaries.

Appendix

I = Internalized   E = Emerging   N = No evidence of the skill   Date: _____

Students	Skills/ Strategies to Assess	Focus	Feeling words	Speech bubbles/ dialogue	Setting details	Leads	Endings	Spacing	Spelling	Periods	Other needs

Assessment, Week of _____ Unit: _____

Students / Unit Skills and/or Strategies										Individualized skill(s) needed

Name _____ Date _____

Name _____ Date _____

_____

_____

_____

_____

_____

_____

_____

_____

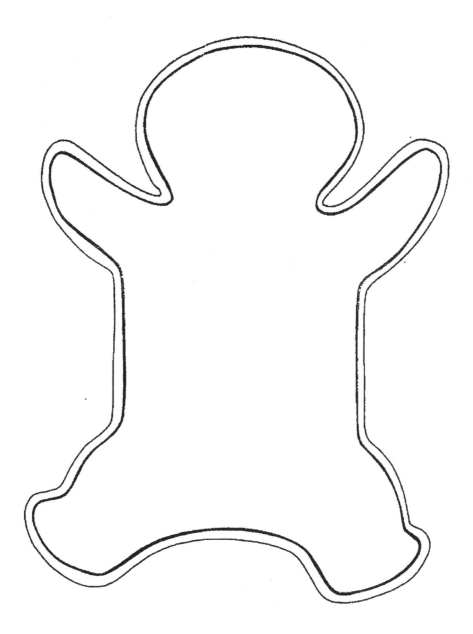

Character: _____

Problems	Solutions

Name _____ Date _____

Beginning	Middle	End

- -

Name _____ Date _____

Part 1	Part 2	Part 3	Part 4

Dear Family,

Over the course of the school year, your child will have the exciting opportunity to write stories and poems and nonfiction books, all on topics of his or her choosing. About once a month, everyone in the class will "publish" a piece of writing, which means that after doing some work to make their drafts better, they will share and celebrate their finished pieces with others.

The writing your child produces in this class will most likely not look like the writing we see in the world. Instead, it will contain developmentally appropriate errors, even when published. Rather than telling students how to spell each word correctly, or editing their pieces and asking them to copy them over with all the periods and capitals in place, I will teach them ways to become more adept themselves at spelling and punctuation. And I will honor their work, errors and all, as a reflection of their best efforts and of their growing knowledge base. Doing so allows students to develop their independence and their confidence as writers as they see and celebrate evidence of their best work, rather than of a piece of writing that looks vaguely like something they worked on once.

Over the course of the school year, instead of noticing the errors in your child's writing, look for the growth. For example, you might look for an evolving knowledge of spelling. Once children begin to write, they usually move through the following stages of spelling development:

1. Children begin by putting random strings of letters on the page.

2. As they learn which letters go with which sounds, they spell by putting down the first letter of each word.

3. Later, they record the first and last letters of each word.

4. Next, children learn to hear sounds throughout a word, recording beginning, middle, and end letters that correspond with those sounds. We call this work "invented spelling" because it emerges from children's knowledge of phonics. For example, instead of writing "different" a child might write "diffrint." Or if a child's pronunciation of the "th" sound sounds more like a "d," she might write "the" as "da."

5. Finally, children consistently use conventional spelling. (Leading up to this stage, children will intersperse invented spellings with conventional spellings.)

If you're looking for ways to help your child with his or her writing, you might brainstorm topics together. Or you might help your child orally tell you exactly what he or she wants to write, and then encourage the child to do the best he or she can to get down on the page the pictures and words (even if those "words" are random strings of letters) that will convey what he or she said. I can also talk with you about additional ways you might support your child based on his or her specific stage of development.

I am very much looking forward to helping and watching your child grow as a writer!

Sincerely,

Professional Resources

Anderson, C. (2000). *How's it going? A practical guide to conferring with student writers.* Portsmouth, NH: Heinemann.

Angelillo, J. (2002). *A fresh approach to teaching punctuation: Helping young writers use conventions with precision and purpose.* New York: Scholastic.

Bender, J. (2007). *The resourceful writing teacher: A menu of essential skills and strategies.* Portsmouth, NH: Heinemann.

Bernays, A., and Painter, P. (1995). *What if? Writing exercises for fiction writers.* New York: Longman.

Butler, A., and Turbill, J. (1987). *Towards a reading-writing classroom.* Portsmouth, NH: Heinemann.

Cambourne, B. (1995). Toward an educationally relevant theory of literacy learning: Twenty years of inquiry. *The Reading Teacher,* Vol. 49, No. 3.

Common core state standards for English language arts & literacy in history/social studies, science, and technical subjects (2010). Washington, D.C.: Common Core Standards Initiative.

Dousis, A. (November 2008). Lively and artful sharings. *The Responsive Classroom Newsletter,* Vol. 20, No. 4.

McCarrier, A, Pinnell, G., and Fountas, I. (1999). *Interactive writing: How language & literacy come together, K–2.* Portsmouth, NH: Heinemann.

McKenzie, M.G. (1986). *Journeys into literacy.* Huddersfield, England: Schofield & Sims.

Peck, R.N. (1983). *Fiction is folks: How to create unforgettable characters.* Cincinnati: Writer's Digest Books.

Smith, F. (1994). *Writing and the writer* (second edition). Hillsdale, NJ: Lawrence Erlbaum Associates.

Vygotsky, L.S., edited by Cole, M., John-Steiner, V., Scribner, S., and Souberman, E. (1978). *Mind in society. The development of higher psychological processes.* Cambridge, MA: Harvard University Press.

Children's Literature

Al Abdullah, Her Majesty Queen Rania. (2010). *The sandwich swap.* New York: Hyperion Books.

Bang, Molly. (1999). *When Sophie gets angry—really, really angry . . .* New York: Scholastic.

Brallier, Jess M. (2001). *Tess's tree.* New York: HarperCollins Children's Books.

Brinckloe, Julie. (1985). *Fireflies!* New York: Aladdin Paperbacks.

Brisson, Pat. (2006). *Melissa Parkington's beautiful, beautiful hair.* Honesdale, PA: Boyds Mill Press.

Brown, Peter. (2009). *The curious garden.* New York: Little, Brown and Company.

Bunting, Eve. (1991). *Fly away home.* New York: Clarion Books.

_____. (2006). *One green apple.* New York: Clarion Books.

Burke, Tina. (2007). *Sophie's big bed.* La Jolla, CA: Kane/Miller Book Publishers.

Castellucci, Cecil. (2010). *Grandma's gloves.* Somerville, MA: Candlewick Press.

Cole, Henry. (2007). *On Meadowview Street.* New York: Scholastic.

Crews, Donald. (1992). *Shortcut.* New York: Greenwillow Books.

DePaola, Tomie. (1979). *Oliver Button is a sissy.* Orlando, FL: Voyager Books.

Graham, Bob. (2008). *How to heal a broken wing.* Cambridge, MA: Candlewick Press.

Henkes, Kevin. (1985). *Bailey goes camping*. New York: Greenwillow Books.

_____. (1989). *Jessica*. New York: Greenwillow Books.

_____. (2003). *Julius's candy corn*. New York: HarperFestival.

_____. (2004). *Lilly's chocolate heart*. New York: HarperFestival.

_____. (1993). *Owen*. New York: Greenwillow Books.

_____ . (1993). *Sheila Rae's peppermint stick*. New York: HarperFestival.

_____ . (1987). *Sheila Rae the Brave*. New York: Greenwillow Books.

Hoffman, Mary. (1991). *Amazing Grace*. New York: Dial Books for Young Readers.

Howe, James. (2002). *Horace and Morris join the chorus (but what about Dolores?)*. New York: Atheneum Books for Young Readers.

Jahn-Clough, Lisa. (1999). *My friend and I*. Boston: Houghton Mifflin Company.

Javaherbin, Mina. (2010). *Goal!* Somerville, MA: Candlewick Press.

Keats, Ezra Jack. (1969). *Goggles*. New York: Puffin Books.

_____. (1998). *A letter to Amy*. New York: Viking.

_____. (1967). *Peter's chair*. New York: Puffin Books.

Kooser, Ted. (2010). *Bag in the wind*. Somerville, MA: Candlewick Press.

Krauss, Ruth. (1945). *The carrot seed*. New York: Scholastic.

Lee, Suzy. (2008). *Wave*. San Francisco: Chronicle Books.

Michelson, Richard. (2010). *Busing Brewster.* New York: Alfred A. Knopf.

Moulton, Mark Kimball. (2010). *The very best pumpkin.* New York: Simon Schuster Books for Young Readers.

Naylor, Phyllis Reynolds. (1991). *King of the playground*. New York: Aladdin Paperbacks.

Partridge, Elizabeth. (2003). *Whistling*. New York: Greenwillow Books.

Rankin, Laura. (2007). *Ruthie and the (not so) teeny tiny lie*. New York: Bloomsbury Children's Books.

Rathman, Peggy. (1991). *Ruby and the copycat*. New York: Scholastic.

Reynolds, Peter H. (2004). *Ish*. Cambridge, MA: Candlewick Press.

_____. (2003). *The dot.* Cambridge, MA: Candlewick Press.

Rodman, Mary Ann. (2005). *My best friend*. London: Puffin Books.

Rousaki, Maria. (2003). *Unique Monique*. La Jolla, CA : Kane/Miller Book Publishers.

Rylant, Cynthia. (1987; 1990; 1997). Henry and Mudge series. New York: Aladdin Books; London: Collier Macmillan; New York: Bradbury Press; New York: Simon & Schuster Books for Young Readers.

_____. (1996). *The old woman who named things*. San Diego: Harcourt Brace.

Simont, Marc. (2001). *The stray dog*. New York: Scholastic.

Slobodkina, Esphyr. (1940). *Caps for Sale*. New York: W. R. Scott Inc.

Viorst, Judith. (1971). *The tenth good thing about Barney*. New York: Atheneum.

Waber, Bernard. (1972). *Ira sleeps over.* Boston: Houghton Mifflin.

Wells, Rosemary. (1997). *Bunny cakes*. New York: Dial Books for Young Readers.

_____. (1981). *Timothy goes to school.* New York: Viking.

Willems, Mo. (2004). *Knuffle Bunny: A cautionary tale*. New York: Hyperion Books for Children.

_____. (2010). *Knuffle Bunny free*. New York: Hyperion Books for Children.

_____. (2007). *Knuffle Bunny too: A case of mistaken identity*. New York: Hyperion Books for Children.

Zolotow, Charlotte. (1966). *Big sister and little sister*. New York: HarperTrophy.

_____. (1972). *William's doll.* New York: HarperCollins Publishers.